Amen! This book ought to be requi.... ..au.ng in every seminary, diocesan office, and ministry program. With the heart of a pastor and three decades of experience fostering the gifts of the baptized, Bishop Clark celebrates the call of lay ecclesial ministers and challenges the whole Church to move forward in hope.

Edward P. Hahnenberg, PhD
Author of *Ministries: A Relational Approach*

Forward in Hope is an example of how theological reflection and the test of experience shows the value of time, which has allowed the seeds of Vatican II to sprout beautifully where they have been watered by the Holy Spirit. The growth has not been uniform or even universal and, in some parts of the church, it has been met with reluctance and even opposition. The book is excellent and needed.

Bishop Anthony G. Bosco
Bishop Emeritus of Greensburg

Every parishioner should read this highly intelligent and inspiring book, which chronicles an exciting development within our church—lay ecclesial ministry. Bishop Clark believes in the one *ministerium* of all those called to ministry (ordained and lay), and gives readers an idea of what that looks like with the presentation of lay voices along with his own. *Forward in Hope* is a marvel of pastoral clarity, sensitivity and episcopal leadership on a current, though still controversial topic.

Karen Sue Smith
Editorial Director
America

In this inspiring volume a bishop and his people offer a remarkable testimony to the work of the Spirit in the recovery of a form of ministry that goes back to the very origins of the church. Bishop Clark eloquently demonstrates the possibility of a fruitful collaboration between ordained and lay ecclesial ministry in the service of the Church.

Richard R. Gaillardetz, PhD
Murray/Bacik Professor of Catholic Studies
University of Toledo

Here we meet a courageous bishop, well grounded in the history of the Church, fully aware of the challenges of the present moment, and yet hopeful about the emerging future. Clark prods his fellow bishops, but also all of us, to welcome with open arms one of the most significant movements of the Spirit in our time.

Ann M. Garrido
Author of *A Concise Guide to Supervising a Ministry Student*

This book is more than an "Amen" to Lay Ecclesial Ministry. Its reflections highlight a long tradition of lay leadership in the Church. This book brings to life what Pope Benedict says about the laity being co-responsible with priests in the life of a parish in particular.

Rev. John E. Hurley, C.S.P.
Former Executive Director,
National Pastoral Life Center

FORWARD
H*in*OPE

Saying *AMEN*
to Lay
Ecclesial Ministry

Bishop
MATTHEW H. CLARK

ave maria press notre dame, indiana

Founded in 1865, Ave Maria Press is a ministry of the Indiana Province of Holy Cross.

www.avemariapress.com

ISBN-10 1-59471-191-7   ISBN-13 978-1-59471-191-6

Cover image © Design Pics Inc. / Alamy.

Cover and text design by John R. Carson.

Printed and bound in the United States of America.

Library of Congress Cataloging-in-Publication Data

Clark, Matthew H.
  Forward in hope : saying amen to lay ecclesial ministry / by Matthew H. Clark.
     p. cm.
  ISBN-13: 978-1-59471-191-6 (pbk.)
  ISBN-10: 1-59471-191-7 (pbk.)
  1. Lay ministry--Catholic Church--History. I. Title.
  BX1920.C525 2009
  262'.152--dc22
                            2009032992

To the people of the Diocese of Rochester,
and to my co-workers in the vineyard, lay and ordained,
who serve them so lovingly and generously.

To Mary Ann —
a servant of
other ; of our
of mission.

Peace

[signature]
12/26/0?

Let us go forward in hope! A new millennium is opening before the Church like a vast ocean upon which we shall venture, relying on the help of Christ. The Son of God, who became incarnate two thousand years ago out of love for humanity, is at work even today: we need discerning eyes to see this and, above all, a generous heart to become the instruments of his work.

—Pope John Paul II
Novo Millennio Ineunte, 58

Contents

Foreword

History is long, perhaps in the Catholic Church even longer than otherwise, and its perspectives emerge slowly. In this volume, Bishop Matthew Clark presents his own insights about lay ecclesial ministry. These are drawn from the rich personal experience of one who has intimately lived with its historical unfolding, indeed, in his role as bishop, providing leadership for its development. In the telling, we learn much about lay ecclesial ministry and about Bishop Clark, as well as about individual lay ecclesial ministers from his diocese. The encounters are enriching intellectually and spiritually, and give ample evidence of why the title of this volume is *Forward in Hope*.

First, a reflection on the history that is explored. Beginning with scripture, and moving deftly through particular moments of Church history, key developments that led to the evolution of the understandings of ministry prevalent before Vatican II are presented with brevity and clarity. The theological assessment is that, at various junctures in the story, change was suitable for its time, and incremental. The central role of the Second Vatican Council is explored at greater length, with the added dimension of the personal experience of then-seminarian Matthew Clark, his excitements, and hesitations. The most recent history focuses on some papal writing and the document of the United States Conference of Catholic Bishops, *Co-Workers in the Vineyard of the Lord.* This approach effectively situates the development of lay ecclesial ministry within the unfolding tradition of the Church.

However, there is a more personal historical telling here— that of Bishop Clark's first encounter with lay ecclesial ministry in Rochester, New York, after his installation as bishop, and his ongoing work with this new aspect of ministry in the Church. It is clear in the account that he paid careful attention to the lay women and men serving in his parishes, to the pastors and priests working with them, to the faculty at St. Bernard's Seminary who prepared many in their Master of Divinity program, and to the people of his parishes. On the one hand, he speaks of his efforts to discern what the work of the Spirit is, and of his conclusion based on his encounter with "the grace and power of lay ministry" that the emergence of what we now call lay ecclesial ministry is indeed precisely that. On the other hand, he is sensitive to the concerns of some priests, indeed, some fellow bishops, on whose cautionary comments he reflects. His assessment is realistic, recognizing the various challenges facing the Church, yet most positive, saying that lay ecclesial ministry is "a sign of true renewal and hope."

Second, a reflection on Bishop Clark. In his telling of his own story, we meet this priest, bishop, spiritual pilgrim. It is clear that he has a deep loyalty to the Church, both the universal Church of history and today, and the particular Church of Rochester. The latter is demonstrated in his attitude of listening—the account of his effort to come to know his people when he first came to the diocese as bishop is one example; the listening sessions with lay ecclesial ministers in preparation for the writing of this book another, ever striving "to be open to the truth." It is also evident that at times this listening is painful, both in the carrying of the pain felt, for example, by pastoral administrators, from the ambiguities present in their roles, and in the struggle with pastoral decisions deemed necessary in the face of what is learned of the people's needs relative to the official Church's positions. At times, his reflections become a powerful *apologia*. A central theme in his assessment of developments in ministry today, and clearly in his own life, is that of communion. He speaks of the importance of "faithful relationships among the ministers of the Gospel" and the importance of living "fully in the community of the Church." Furthermore, he stresses the importance of structures of communion, and gives as an example the *ministerium* of priests, deacons, and lay ecclesial ministers of his diocese. A theology of communion, a spirituality of communion, and practical steps toward communion are each carefully explored.

The subtitle of this volume is *Saying* Amen *to Lay Ecclesial Ministry*. *Webster's* states that *amen* is "used to express solemn ratification . . . or hearty approval." Indeed, Bishop Clark offers such approval in this book, such ratification in his diocese. *The Harper Collins Encyclopedia of Catholicism* adds further perspective: "Amen, word said as the formal conclusion to liturgical prayer. Uttering the word constitutes the acceptance of a claim." In light of the context of discernment within which lay ecclesial ministry is explored by Bishop Clark and the sense he proffers of the need to move toward a more just inclusion of these new ministers within the ordered ministries of the Church, his *amen* is clearly from the heart.

Zeni Fox, PhD
Immaculate Conception Seminary
Seton Hall University

Introduction

When I was asked to offer a book of my own reflections on lay ecclesial ministry, I accepted with some trepidation. The growth in numbers of lay ecclesial ministers in the United States has been astounding, with more than 30,000 now working in a wide variety of pastoral settings. Many of these are full-time professional ministers; many others are employed part-time. While their presence as paid members of parish and diocesan staffs reaches every corner of the nation, it has not been without some controversy and deep concern among the Catholic bishops of the United States and among other members of the clergy and the laity. This phenomenon has surfaced new doctrinal, theological, pastoral, and administrative challenges. The meaning, contexts, and distinctions of baptismal and ordained ministries, requirements for formation and accountability, the acceptance of lay ecclesial ministers in the life and mission of the Church, fair employment practices, just compensation, and matters related to due process are but a few of the issues with which we Catholics now must grapple as we seek to incorporate lay people working in professional Church ministries.

I remember vividly the moment when the late Cardinal Avery Dulles stood to address the United States Conference of Catholic Bishops in November 2005, a gathering I must say that was not in full agreement with the draft of the document before us—*Co-Workers in the Vineyard of the Lord: A Resource for Guiding the Development of Lay Ecclesial Ministry* (*CWVL*).

The stated purpose of *Co-Workers* was "to be a common frame of reference for ensuring that the development of lay ecclesial ministry continues in ways that are faithful to the Church's theological and doctrinal tradition and that responds to contemporary pastoral needs and situations" (*CWVL*, p. 6).

In the midst of my brother bishops' deep discussion over what exactly "ministry" is and whether or not the term can or should be associated with people who are not ordained, Cardinal Dulles rose to the floor. He spoke very strongly that such use of the word *ministry* was not a new development for the Church but rather has been part of our tradition for centuries. He spoke eloquently, as always, that we shouldn't fear using this kind of language about the laity, that this seemingly brand-new thing was not new at all.

While I cannot document it, it was my own perception and that of several other bishops to whom I spoke afterward that the intervention by this man—who commanded so much admiration and respect—made all the difference in what still ended up a very close vote to approve *Co-Workers* by the required two-thirds majority. The final vote was one hundred ninety for and forty-nine against, with five abstentions.

I add my own thoughts about lay ecclesial ministry here in this book because I am convinced, based on more than three decades of experience with this ministry by people in our own Diocese of Rochester, that this is a work of the Holy Spirit; that we can embrace the growth as beneficial to our parishes, dioceses, and the universal Church; and that encouraging lay people to serve the Church in this special way is a fulfillment of the promise and spirit of the Second Vatican Council. I have included in this book essays by five lay ecclesial ministers working in my diocese, which I am calling "Voices from the Vineyard." I believe their experiences and thoughts, and the thoughts and experiences of thousands of others like them

across the country, will help us better understand this development that is still flowering, still in its infancy.

At the L. J. McGinley lecture at Fordham University in
2006, Cardinal Dulles laid out the promise and the challenge
inherent in the growth of lay ecclesial ministry in the Church
today.

> Ours is not a time for rivalry between clergy and
> laity, or between lay ministers and apostles to the
> world, as if what was given to the one were taken
> away from the other. Only through cooperation
> among all her members can the Church live up to
> her divine calling. Just as the eye cannot say to the
> ear, "I have no need of you," so the lay minister
> and the social reformer, the contemplative religious
> and the parish priest must say to each other: "I
> need your witness and assistance to discern and
> live up to my own vocation in the Body of Christ."
> Because the lay faithful constitute the overwhelm-
> ing majority of Catholics, the future of the Church
> lies predominantly in their hands. The recognition
> recently given to lay ecclesial ministries should help
> the laity to rise to the challenges and opportunities
> that are theirs today.

I agree wholeheartedly with Cardinal Dulles. At the same
time, I recognize and wish to discuss here the theological and
practical issues in my own diocese and in the wider Church
that remain more than forty years after a pastor in one of our
diocesan parishes hired a religious woman to be his pastoral
assistant, fully involved in the ministry of the Church. I believe
this appointment, made well before I arrived in Rochester,
was among the first in the nation and soon led to other pastors hiring lay people to assist them. St. Bernard's Seminary in
Rochester established a master of divinity degree in 1969 and
allowed non-seminarians to enroll. This professional degree,

once reserved solely for those preparing for ordination, was now available to help prepare those who embraced a call to lay ecclesial ministry as a vocation. It may well have been the first Roman Catholic seminary in the United States to do so.

The questions and concerns expressed by my brother bishops in our discussion of whether *Co-Workers in the Vineyard of the Lord* would be approved remain.

- What exactly are lay ecclesial ministers?
- What is their relationship to the ordained?
- Are they a threat to the authority of priests?
- What is and should be their relationship with the local bishop?
- How do we adequately prepare them for their work and commission them for service?
- From where do they draw their authority?

These questions and concerns are genuine, posed by those who are wary of the development of lay ecclesial ministry no less than those who, like me, fully support the ongoing infusion of highly trained lay people into the daily ministry of the Church in support of our mission. Indeed, these are legitimate and necessary questions and issues that must be part of the ongoing discernment of this old, yet new development in the life of the Catholic Church. These are questions that all of us who love the Church must address.

Acknowledging that there is worry, caution, and even resistance among some of the ordained and good and faithful lay people—including in my own diocese—how do we better communicate and explain the role of the lay ecclesial minister and their place in the Church?

- What does it mean to the individual and to the Church that lay ecclesial ministers express almost universally a "call from God"; and how can we discern, honor, sustain,

and nurture that call and remain faithful to our ecclesial tradition?

- How do we balance our efforts to stem and reverse the
  decline in the number of priestly vocations with the
  exponential growth of lay ecclesial ministry?
- Need these two developments be at odds with one
  another?

Co-Workers in the Vineyard of the Lord, above all, says
we need to build carefully. It is neither the complete nor the
last word on this development. It does not carry the force of
Church law but is intended as a guide to further development,
a challenge to trust the activity of the Holy Spirit, and a call
to enduring hope. The document concludes in part with these
words:

> The same God who called Prisca and Aquila to
> work with Paul in the first century calls thousands
> of men and women to minister in our Church in
> the twenty-first century. This is a cause for rejoic-
> ing. It also is an occasion for the kind of planning
> that Pope John Paul II recommended in *Novo Mil-
> lennio Ineunte*:
>
> > The program already exists: it is the plan
> > found in the Gospel and in the living tradition;
> > it is the same as ever. Ultimately, it has its center
> > in Christ himself, who is to be known, loved and
> > imitated, so that in him we may live the life of the
> > Trinity, and with him transform history until its
> > fulfillment in the heavenly Jerusalem.
> > —*Co-Workers in the Vineyard of the Lord,* p. 66

I firmly believe that we need to be trusting. We need to
be confident that the Lord is guiding us and that we will find
our way through whatever issues are currently with us or may
arise in the future. I believe *Co-Workers* overall says "amen" to

the development thus far and is an expression of confidence that what is well begun will continue to grow, realistic in acknowledging that we are not all in the same place around the country. I also believe without reservation that we must proceed with due diligence but without fear. My experience has vividly revealed to me the beauty of this development and how deeply it is enriching our daily lives as Catholics.

I believe that we can move forward, confident that we have five important pillars of truth on which to base our hope. These pillars, which I outline below, frame the conversation about lay ecclesial ministry in today's Church that I explore further in the pages of this book.

1. The idea of lay ecclesial ministry as we now define it connects us in an authentic and fruitful manner with the very earliest traditions of the Church.

The New Testament bears witness to the broad involvement of the baptized in the various works of the budding Church. This ancient embrace of ministry by the baptized in service to the Christian community was recalled and re-appropriated for our own time by the Second Vatican Council. *Lumen Gentium* (*LG*) affirms that the mission of the Church resides with all the faithful, not just with the ordained hierarchy. Further, it affirms that all members of the Church are called to holiness in Christ Jesus. This is explicitly outlined in the decree on the laity. It was, however, *Sacrosanctum Concilium*, the Constitution on the Sacred Liturgy (*SC*) that perhaps more than any other document laid the foundation for the renewed theology of ministry by proclaiming that the work of liturgy flows from the full, active, and conscious participation of all the faithful (*SC*, 14). Pope Paul VI reiterated this renewed theology of ministry in 1975 as the Church was just beginning to assimilate the teachings of Vatican II.

The laity can also feel called, or in fact be called, to cooperate with their pastors in the service of the ecclesial community, for the sake of its growth and life. This can be done through the exercise of different kinds of ministries according to the grace and charisms that the Lord has been pleased to bestow on them.

—*On Evangelization in the Modern World*, 73

2. As we experience it in our parishes now, lay ecclesial ministry is very much in keeping with the spirit of Vatican II and the re-igniting by the Council of the idea that by our baptism all of us—not just the ordained—are called to build up the community of the Church for the transformation of the world.

The Risen Lord calls everyone to labor in his vineyard, that is, in a world that must be transformed in view of the final coming of the Reign of God; and the Holy Spirit empowers all with the various gifts and ministries for the building up of the Body of Christ.

—*Co-Workers in the Vineyard of the Lord*, p. 7

By offering their God-provided gifts to grow the Kingdom, lay people must work in unison with the ordained, not as passive receivers of God's grace but as conduits of it.

3. Nothing in our tradition or teachings of the magisterium suggests that lay ecclesial ministry is intended to be a replacement for or a substitute for the ministry of the ordained. This is absolute.

The primary distinction lies between the ministry of the lay faithful and the ministry of the ordained, which is a special apostolic calling. Both are rooted

in sacramental initiation, but the pastoral ministry
of the ordained is empowered in a unique and
essential way by the sacrament of Holy Orders.
Through it, the ministry of the apostles is extended.
As successors to the apostles, bishops "with priests
and deacons as helpers" shepherd their dioceses as
"teachers of doctrine, priests for sacred worship,
and ministers of government" (*LG*, 20). This recognition of the unique role of the ordained is not
a distinction based on merit or rank; rather, it is
a distinction based on the sacramental character
given by the Holy Spirit that configures the recipi-
ent to Christ the Head and on the particular relationship of service that Holy Orders brings about
between ecclesiastical ministry and the community.
The ordained ministry is uniquely constitutive of
the Church in a given place. All other ministries
function in relation to it.

—*Co-Workers in the Vineyard
of the Lord*, p. 21

*4. Lay ecclesial ministry, carried forth as an embodiment of our
deepest traditions and carefully integrated into the life of our
Church, is a rich help and not a hindrance to our priests.*

The presence of and growth in numbers of lay ecclesial ministers should be viewed as a complement to the ministry of the
ordained and not as corrosive of their authority or place in the
Church.

One of the chief questions asked by both lay ecclesial
ministers and the people in the pews is, "If there is a substantial increase in the number of priests in coming years, will we
still need lay ecclesial ministers?" My answer is a resounding
yes! I share the convictions of Cardinal Roger Mahoney, archbishop of Los Angeles, in this regard.

It must be recognized that lay ministry rooted in the priesthood of the baptized is not a stopgap measure. Even if seminaries were once again filled to overflowing and convents packed with sisters, there would still remain the need for cultivating, developing, and sustaining the full flourishing of ministries that we have witnessed in the Church since the Second Vatican Council. In the wake of the council, we have arrived at a clearer recognition that it is in the nature of the Church to be endowed with many gifts, and that these gifts are the basis for the vocations to the priesthood, the diaconate, and the religious life, as well as for the many ministries rooted in the call of baptism.

—Cardinal Roger Mahoney
As I Have Done For You: A Pastoral Letter on Ministry, Part Two

Additionally, it is helpful to remind ourselves that the first bishops' commission on lay ministry was established in 1962, a time when seminaries and novitiates were, in fact, overflowing. Lay ministry was not then and is not now seen as a stopgap or a "help Father" issue; it is a pastoral development and theological insight in its own right.

Even so, with no significant sign that the gradual decline in the number of priests will abate soon, the presence of lay ecclesial ministers will allow us to sustain our parishes and serve more people than we could without their presence. In my own diocese, I have seen this repeatedly. The presence of our lay ecclesial ministers in nearly every facet of our mission extends what we can do, not only numerically but also in terms of the unique gifts and contributions lay ecclesial ministers bring to the Church.

5. We simply could not do what we do without lay ecclesial ministers. The ideas, energy, and creativity they have and continue to offer simply cannot be replaced.

This is not just a statement about the fact that we need people to provide ministry in the Church, but an honest recognition of what these lay ecclesial ministers have brought to our parishes and diocesan ministries. They add not only their able hands to the work of the Lord, but so much more. Their depth of life experience enriches and inspires our parishioners. Those who are married often bring a special sensitivity to women and men who share that vocation. They can relate closely with other married people and give those who need it relevant help and good counsel. They can offer their experiences or use what they have learned in their own homes to lead and inspire others. They supplement and enrich the holiness of the Church even as their souls are nourished by the very ministry to which they are called.

There is a variety of ways in which lay ministers serve the Church today. On the one hand there are lay ministers who serve in primarily volunteer roles and whose service is limited to a relatively small number of hours each week. These include extraordinary ministers of the Eucharist, lectors, cantors, choir members, catechists, visitors of the sick, outreach workers, sacramental preparation instructors, youth ministers, and justice outreach program participants.

And there are also those who serve on a more permanent basis and for much more time each week. These people hold paid ecclesial positions; working at least twenty hours each week; many if not most, of them hold full-time positions. These are the ministries whose authority appropriately comes from the bishop rather than the pastor himself. These people undergo ministerial formation and are charged with leading others and collaborating directly with ordained ministers.

They include pastoral administrators or directors of parish life, pastoral associates, catechetical leaders, youth ministry leaders, school principals, and directors of liturgy and pastoral music. By 2005 there were over thirty thousand lay people in this second category alone.

I offer in this book my personal thoughts on lay ecclesial ministry and stories from my thirty years experience as bishop, forty-seven as a priest, and a lifetime of being a Catholic because I believe we can build a better understanding and wise embrace of lay ecclesial ministry. I also believe the challenges are many, but quite surmountable if we but approach the challenges with the same fresh energy and creativity that the late Holy Father John Paul II called for at the close of the Great Jubilee Year 2000, in *Novo Millennio Ineunte*, "Let us go forward in hope!"

1

One Bishop's Story

I am certain that the growth of my understanding and appreciation of the expansion of lay ministry in the Church is, in large part, a direct result of my pastoral experience as Bishop of Rochester. When I remember the night of my installation as the eighth bishop of this diocese, I am powerfully reminded that that celebration was a pivotal moment in my life. When I remember the night, I am aware of the powerful formative influence the priests, religious, and lay faithful of Rochester have had in my life and growth.

The Catholic people of Rochester were, and remain now, a people who are strong in their faith—ready and willing to live and celebrate it through service to God and neighbor. I know that this does not make them unique. I know that the people of many other dioceses could be described in the same way. But, I also know that every diocese has its own distinct personality. Each claims the same faith; but no two understand it, live it, and share it in exactly the same way. Had I been assigned back then to Portland or Harrisburg or Wilmington, I would certainly have been shaped and molded in wonderful ways through my experiences with the Catholic faithful in those places. But it would not have been in just the same way as it happened here. That interplay, that sharing of life and common growth is part of the Church's ancient wisdom that the relationship between a bishop and his diocese is analogous in some ways to the spousal relationship. My concrete and practical exposure to the issues surrounding the emergence of lay ministry in the Diocese of Rochester is a prime example of this.

When I arrived in Rochester in 1979 as their newly appointed bishop, I brought with me my own personality, gifts, and set of personal and ministerial experiences that made me who I was at that time. My only experience of Rochester until then was two years of philosophy at Saint Bernard's Seminary from 1957 to 1959. I enjoyed happy reunions with fellow students when I returned twenty years later but had very little firsthand knowledge of the diocese. Additionally, I was keenly aware at the time that my ministerial experience prior to my appointment as bishop was not typical of what one might expect to find on the curriculum vitae of a candidate for that office.

I had never been a pastor and had been a full-time parish priest for only two years. My other assignments included a year teaching in a high school, canon law studies, an assignment in the chancery and another as priests' personnel director for the Diocese of Albany. Brief as these experiences were, each was rewarding in its own way. Each made me aware that we can bring something of value to any ministry that we approach in a spirit of faith and a desire to serve. But, more importantly, I learned that every ministry entered in that spirit changes the ministers. From those early experiences, there grew in me the disposition to listen for the Lord's voice in whatever ministerial experience into which I was called.

In 1972, I was invited to an assignment that came to be the longest of my priesthood prior to my Episcopal ordination in 1979. That was joining the staff of the North American

College in Rome as spiritual director. I realized when I accepted that assignment that if I was to help the seminarians in
their spiritual development, I had to rededicate myself to my
own spiritual growth and development as well. As those men
were "testing" their call to priesthood, I strove to deepen my
personal commitment to my own spirituality and relationship
to the Lord. Those years were happy and growth-filled: many
thanks to the support of colleagues on the staff; a wonderful
spiritual guide, the late Edward Malatesta, S.J.; and the seminarians whose honesty and openness were great gifts.

At the end of my seven years I was in the happy position
of enjoying what I did, but at the same time looking forward
to a broader kind of ministry at home. I loved the students but
looked forward to serving a wide range of people. As God's
providence would have it, I was called to minister to and
among a wide range of people. It was not to be as presbyter in
Albany, however, but as Bishop of Rochester.

So, on the night of my installation as bishop, I was aware
that my prayers had been answered, even if in a way I had
not anticipated. I knew I was shifting from a ministry with
a very particular focus, with a narrow constituency in terms
of talent, gender, and mode of engagement in the Church, to
the breadth and scope of a progressive, energetic diocese that
had already opened itself to many of the reforms called for by
Vatican Council II. Quite consciously aware that I had never
served as pastor, I was deeply challenged by the call that I
now had to be the chief pastor of an entire, and wonderfully
vibrant, diocese.

Based on my experience of the lessons and gifts to be
found in every ministerial experience, I knew that in order to
be able to offer leadership to the community I needed to learn
its story and become familiar with its unfolding pastoral life.
I needed to immerse myself in its history, in the struggles that

had formed it, in the ethos and culture—both ecclesial and civil—that had come to characterize its life and spirit.

I had to learn about the twelve counties of New York State which composed this particular Church—not only its cities and towns, its long and beautiful Finger Lakes, sparkling waterfalls, broad river valleys, rich farm land, beautiful vineyards, and orchards—but also about its women. I discovered early on that in the very center of this diocese, at Seneca Falls, Elizabeth Cady Stanton, Susan B. Anthony, and a host of other women and men called a Women's Rights Convention in 1848, which began the worldwide women's movement. These creative women pushed for a radical rethinking of domestic, educational, political, social, and Church life, all of which had marginalized women. This ferment was translated locally into the founding of a score of female educational institutions, which survive today and continue to influence the local culture to a marked degree.

In addition to a deep desire to learn a great deal about this community, I brought with me a commitment to the Church and a longing to serve it well. I yearned to help this new-to-me diocese continue implementing the values of the Second Vatican Council. It was the people—the priests, the religious, and the lay faithful—who helped me do both. The Catholic people of Rochester were willing to share their stories with me. They were eager to help meet the pastoral challenges of the day and always willing to challenge and question as we moved forward.

I could see almost immediately that this Church liked what they were doing and were satisfied with the direction the diocese was taking. They had appreciated very much the leadership of my predecessors—Archbishop Fulton J. Sheen, who wanted to implement all of the recommendations of the Second Vatican Council in rapid fashion, and Bishop Joseph

L. Hogan, who had been very much engaged in the formation and education of the laity.

My strong impression was that the people expected a similar kind of commitment and involvement from me. They called on me at every turn to explain what I was thinking and the reasons behind my actions. I remember that I thought I had to tread lightly in these discussions, given the sensitivity of some issues and the high level of expectation they had for me.

I also knew that I had to test all of their and my convictions in light of the teaching of our tradition. All of this sharpened my awareness that, ultimately, I had to determine my own style and priorities of leadership. I could not act out of a desire to please or to avoid problems or conflict.

My arrival in Rochester generated much curiosity and concern. Remember, I had arrived there from Rome! People in all walks of the Church wanted to know, "Would the new bishop support what had evolved locally?" Or, did he have orders to put the lid on things? It became clear early on that there had been significant emphasis placed on the emerging role for women in this diocese. One of the expectations among some was that the ordination of women would soon be approved by the Church. They saw this as a natural outgrowth of the fact that, already, women held significant positions in the diocese and in many of our parishes. I remember being peppered so often with such questions about the issue that I thought it would be helpful to put my thoughts on the ministry of women in writing. The task of doing so would force me to express in some clear and systematic way what I thought about these issues. I also thought that what I wrote would be strengthened if it was written with as much input as possible from the community. Thus, the controversial issue of ordination provided an important moment for our local Church.

The wonderful conversations generated by this writing effort produced "The Fire in the Thornbush: A Pastoral Letter on Women in the Church and Society," which we published on April 29, 1982, the Feast of St. Catherine of Siena. The process leading to the publication of this document, and the document itself, have proven to be useful in our diocese. This is true in terms of our efforts to appreciate Pope Paul VI's teaching on the ordination of women and further developments surrounding the ordination question. But, it is also true in terms of our desire to understand and to build on the most helpful patterns of an emerging lay ministry. Even at that early date, and having only recently arrived in Rochester, I could sense that the evolving role of the laity would be a matter of significant attention in the years ahead.

> When we think of women and of all the laity in relation to this work of Christ, we realize that there is much that needs to be made more explicit, more open and more inclusive. Vatican Council II affirmed that pastors have the "duty to shepherd the faithful and recognize their ministries and charisms so that all, according to their proper roles, may cooperate in this common undertaking with one heart" For from Christ "the whole body, being close joined and knit together through every joint of the system, according to the functioning in due measure of each single part derives its increase to the building of itself in love" [Eph 4:16] (*LG*, 30).
>
> The Fathers of Vatican Council II said of the laity: "They are in their own way made sharers in the priestly, prophetic and kingly functions of Christ; and they carry out their own part in the mission of the whole Christian people with respect to the Church and the world" (*LG*, 31).
>
> The Dogmatic Constitution on the Church was promulgated in November 1964. As we look

back on that document after eighteen years, we find ourselves remembering the many ways in which the Church has translated into its daily practice the meaning of such phrases as "their proper roles," "the functioning in due measure," and "in their own way." At the same time, we struggle to understand how the reality of the present day constantly calls the whole Church to a renewed understanding of her mission which is our "common undertaking."

It is part of our work in this local Church to deepen our understanding of how each of us can become more fully "sharers in the priestly, prophetic and kingly functions of Christ."

For the present there is much which can and should be done to affirm the rights and responsibilities of lay men and women to participate in the teaching, shepherding, and sanctifying work of the Church.

—*The Fire in the Thornbush*, 57–59
Matthew H. Clark, DD, Bishop of Rochester

Since then, I have tried to enjoy and repeat the lessons of consulting about and finally writing that pastoral letter, particularly by engaging people's love of the Lord and love of their Church. Thus, throughout my ministry in Rochester, I have tried to encourage people to share their ideas, hopes, and dreams, and to bring their thinking to the pastoral issues and decisions that we so frequently face.

There seem to be real convictions here in terms of lay ministry. We all realize that something exciting is happening. There is a stirring in the hearts of people, an appreciation of what it is to serve the Lord through pastoral ministry in the name of the Church. We see more and more the fruits and efforts that this call has in their lives. In particular, lay ministers report that they come closer to the Lord as they go deeper into ministry.

Ministry enriches the minister's life because of personal inter-action with others and because of a deepening friendship with the Lord. To hear of this experience is to grow in understand-ing of the grace and power of lay ministry. It also gives birth to the desire to help continue and strengthen the experience.

There has indeed been much strength and many achieve-ments as lay ministry has expanded and flourished. There have also been difficulties and problems. Issues of financing initial and ongoing formation, questions relating to the reception of such ministry by the whole Church, concerns about the peace and unity among ministers of the Gospel all continue to call us to prayer, research, and respectful conversation. In all of this, I have tried to encourage our lay ministers and the people with whom and among whom they serve. We need to realize that this is not a matter of solving a problem and moving on. Rather, we need to realize that the challenge is to appreciate that this is a matter of faithful relationships among all ministers of the Gospel, and of their relationships with the people they are privileged to serve. We need to find ways to deal with the full range of issues and questions raised, drawing on the teaching of the Church, and relying on the strength and insight that come to us through our communion with other local Churches.

Some have asked about how I came to be so confident in my commitment to learning from and responding to the faith-ful people of our diocese as a genuine source of wisdom in my episcopal ministry. I think that in large measure it goes back to a conversation I had a few days after I had been named a bishop. Archbishop Jean Jadot, then Apostolic Delegate to the United States, asked me how I felt about the appointment. I said I was happy about it but had begun to experience some doubts about my qualifications for the work. I told him that I was not a scholar and that I had some reservations about my abilities, training, and experience.

His response to me was simple. He told me to be confident in the Lord's call and to trust in my own gifts for ministry. I'll never forget his words. They didn't forestall moments of doubt and difficult times, but they have always provided an anchor when I was experiencing them.

This advice probably should not have been as surprising to me as it seemed at the time. I had always had a sense that ordination, for example, doesn't make one smarter than he was before. The act of ordination does not make one holier than he was before, but leaves one as a pilgrim with everyone else. A priest or a bishop is also a searcher, a seeker, and a person of faith whose guidance will always be the Gospel, the teaching of the Church, and the well-being and growth of his local community. No one holds all the answers or all the truths. All Catholics, including bishops, have the gift of the Holy Spirit— alive in the Word, the Eucharist, and the community—as the foundation and source of our faith life.

We know that our communities will be less than what God wants them to be if we do not share our gifts. In a community of faith as broad, as ancient, and as complicated as our own, we have to be open to the truth wherever we find it. I think someone in my position could make the mistake of assuming that he has within himself such knowledge of the dogmas of the Church and such an expert ability to apply them, that he doesn't need those around him to understand how to move forward.

Surely faith is a personal relationship with the Lord Jesus as the One who saves and reconciles us to the Father. Thus, it is a wonderful insight to realize that one is not more brilliant than another, one is not more dedicated than someone else, one is not holier than another may be. When we are appointed to lead the community, it is a very challenging experience. You realize that you, as limited and fragile as you are, have become a primary symbol of unity and faith of that community. You

recognize that this will not be realized simply because the
appointment has been made, or because you will it to be so.
Rather, the key is in the invitation to others, issued through
our common commission as baptized people, to live in, to
love, and to serve the Lord as best they can. So how we behave
and speak in the midst of the community, how we learn to
express in our own voice what is available in the community
for the noble purpose to which we are committed, is itself a
communal exercise.

Whether we are bishops or not, we can't do this by ourselves. We live fully in the community of the Church. We can
only continually invite and encourage, bring people together,
urge people to live fully and faithfully the gifts they have for
the Gospel we profess.

I have heard of bishops who apparently resist the use of
the term "lay ministry." I'm not sure what this means in reality. For example, I was recently told about an archbishop who
has urged those in his diocese not to use the term "lay ecclesial
ministry." He thinks the term is misleading and problematic
in a number of ways. At the same time, though, there are real
and concrete signs in that diocese of the emergence of genuine
lay ministry: an education program at the local seminary is
strengthened by diocesan financial support and healthy enroll-
ment, and many parishes employ lay people in a variety of pastoral ministries. While use of the term may not be encouraged,
and the general concept may be under scrutiny, the archbishop
is helping the reality flourish in his archdiocese.

Another potential difficulty could be reflected in the comments of another bishop who complained at one point that lay
ministry is causing a new caste or class system to be created
in our dioceses. I have to say that my own experience has not
at all indicated that a new ranking or class system is emerging among the people I know who are engaged in ministry. It
is rare in my experience to encounter a lay ecclesial minister

who appears to be in ministry for power or prestige. Still, I understand my colleague's concern in terms of the many ways in which our proneness to sin can make all of us vulnerable to temptations to move in that direction.

Another friend once shared with me his concern that affirming lay ecclesial ministry might indicate a diminishment of commitment to recruiting and developing fine priests for the service of the Church. He seemed to indicate that to support one implies a neglect of the other. My own position is quite different from that. I think the mutual support of both highlights and raises the other to new levels. In my thinking, the fullness of Christ is more fully manifest through the support of both. To those who fear that encouraging lay ministry might constitute a threat to the priesthood, I go back to the example of my own transition from life in Rome to life in Rochester.

As I indicated at the beginning of this chapter, in the seven years prior to my ordination as bishop, I had little experience not only of women in the Church, but actually of anyone except males between the ages of twenty-two and twenty-eight years old. While I would say that there were certainly opportunities to enjoy what diversity there was in Rome in those days, I have to admit that I did not find in the seminary setting the kind of richness that I have found in a Church served by women and other lay ministers. I think the same richness and benefit for the whole Church is available as we learn to nurture the vocations of our fine lay ministers.

Early on, I found that I needed to absorb the experience of lay ministry, to reflect on it in order to come to understand and appreciate it. Obviously I came to this new experience as a kind of blank slate in terms of any experience of this dimension of Church life. I wanted to see what the new picture looked like, I wanted to appreciate it and perhaps to promote it, but I had very little personal experience of it at all. I wondered about what I observed in my new situation, asking, "Is this good? Why is this happening?"

I did not detect anything negative in what I saw happening. In fact, I saw that the people reacted positively to lay ministry. I saw broader numbers of people served because such ministry was available. I saw enriching mutual interaction between ordained and lay ministers. I kept being mindful, over and over, of the passage from Matthew's gospel, "By their fruits you will know them" (Mt 7:16). I can honestly say that it became an awesome kind of thing to unpack, to appreciate all that people were putting into lay ministry to make it actually happen.

As I said earlier, I could have gone to another diocese and experienced this in a very different way. I keep wondering now what would have happened to me, who I would have become, if I had not arrived in Rochester. I am quite certain that I would have been changed and built up by the people of any diocese to which I might have been assigned, but speculating in the abstract makes it impossible to go much further than that. This community in Rochester challenged me in some very life-giving ways. It didn't all happen in the first six months, for sure. There was a first intense flash, but what I have really learned has come gradually through this lengthy ministry of more than thirty years in this diocese.

God so often works in and through the relationships we have with one another. In relationships we experience the Gospel alive in the hearts of our companions. This can only bring us closer to the Lord and renew our confidence and our courage. We are not computers. We are human beings who have freedom and the power to choose. We live in a world that is much more complex, more demanding, more difficult than we could ever anticipate. We face scientific and technological advances that can be both promising and frightening. In short, we need to keep searching. We see this most concretely, perhaps, in the sacraments of initiation. These are really just the beginnings of saying "yes" to the Lord, of learning to appreciate his promises to us and to appreciate what the Church represents to us. Here is where we start to find a treasure and a strength in terms of living the life of faith.

As I have come to understand it, the realities of the pastoral situations we face often call all of us to reexamine our own assumptions. Pastoral ministry itself challenges us to be sure that we have not equated our own life experience with the fullness of truth. This is not an easy thing, because in so many ways we want to trust our own experience. But we always have to be open to the possibility that we need to accept a broader reality than the one we are currently living.

I believe that the Church, in the documents of Vatican Council II, and in the post-conciliar documents, called us to this very thing. Through baptism, we rightly claim the universal call to holiness, to constant growth in the Lord. Through baptism, the Church affirms in each of us a capacity to serve in the name of the Lord. We need to constantly challenge the limits of our own experience—our own view of reality. We need to keep asking, "Is there another way to look at this issue? Do we need to take other steps in order to address the problems before us or to assist us in encountering the fullness of the Lord? What does the Church ask or require of us?" I have to say that I am really challenged in terms of trying to understand people who want nothing to change, when life assures us over and over that everything changes. Life is measured, even, in terms of change and growth.

In reflecting back on people's response to Vatican II, I can't help but think that even before the close of the Council and before our awareness of what the changes to Church life would begin to look like, the various dioceses of the United States already had assumed different patterns and personalities. It became clear to me during the years of the Council that we students arriving for studies at the North American College in Rome had all come from seminaries that had impressed upon their students particular sets of interests and perceptions that reflected the strengths of each institution.

I recall, for example, that many students from St. Mary's Seminary in Baltimore were very interested in and excited about matters relating to the Church's liturgy. Students from Saint Joseph's Seminary in New York had a notable interest in the study of scripture. The seminaries, like the dioceses that supported them, had a clear influence in tuning their students in to the issues of the time and to the probable work of the Council.

As young students, we had a deep curiosity about what an ecumenical Council would be like, about what it would decide. We became aware that some were fearful that the Council would shake things up too much. People of this temperament were likely to want to continue with business as usual. Others were insistent that things would have to change in order for us to make the Gospel more relevant to a century that had already endured a depression, two world wars, and deep social, political, economic, and religious shifts. The faculty at the university reflected these same perspectives. It doesn't mean that one group was bad and the other good, but only that there truly was not agreement on the main issues, even going into the Council.

I was ordained a priest in the very month that the first session of the Second Vatican Council concluded, and I have to say that my formation was very much influenced by the deliberations and outcomes of it. I returned to Rome after a year to study canon law and was privileged to be there during the third and fourth sessions. The Council punctuated so much of my own program of preparation for ministry.

When I returned to my home diocese to begin my ministry of priesthood, I learned that most of our priests were avid and enthusiastic about implementing the initiatives of the Council. Some did think these new directions were intrusive and disruptive to the life of the Church they had known and grown to love. For some, I think, there was an attitude of "It will pass. Let's just try to stick it out." I remember at one point there was difficulty in even bringing priests together for retreats, since debate and argument would often prevail and upset the intention of the retreat itself. Parish communities, in large part, took their leads from their pastors. If the pastor was open to the changes and enthusiastic about the new perspectives, parishes seemed to take on that very flavor, and vice versa.

I, myself, recall a sense of excitement about the new possibilities. At the same time, I recall that during that particular era in American history I found focus on the internal life of the Church unusually complicated, even as a priest. This was because we were introducing enormous changes in Church life into the U.S. culture of the 1960s. This seemed only to increase the turmoil that many people felt. The sense of tumult and instability was very real for all of us. After the relatively calm sense of continuity and stability of the 1950s, along came the peace generation, the Vietnam War, the civil rights movement, the sexual revolution, and challenges to authority on almost every level and in every field. It was hard to isolate ecclesial matters and focus on them, and it was difficult even to set a tone in which we could discuss these things in a productive way. We had many diverse opinions in the Church, surrounded by the swirl of the shifting culture itself.

As I say, some people clamored for stability, wanting to rely on the tradition as we had known it and on the expectations they had come to understand, anticipate, and appreciate. Others were convinced that the Church and its ministers had to be in closer dialogue with the surrounding culture. They wanted to incarnate the Gospel in a particular place and to be open to truth wherever it could be found—from within the tradition and even beyond it.

This was a real challenge at the time. Some people thrived on that challenge. It stimulated their intellectual curiosity and encouraged their desire for a Church that would become a more participatory community. But others resisted anything that touched cherished ways of life. Even our understanding of the Eucharist became part of the discussion. Much of the theology emanating from the Council stressed the Eucharist as food, with the metaphor of the meal prevailing over earlier understandings that relied on the metaphor of sacrifice. It led me to recall my early catechetical instruction to never chew the host out of deference to its sacredness. The shift toward a new understanding, in just this one example, shook Catholicism to its very core.

Even for me personally, there was a sense in which I was not entirely enthusiastic about change. I would judge myself then to be more conservative about Church matters than I am now. It wasn't because I intentionally accepted or ignored arguments on either side of the questions, but I appreciated very much the habits of the life in which I had grown up. I wanted to continue that and carry it forward. I didn't oppose the Council in any *a priori* way; I think I just needed at that point to be shown—I needed to have the new theologies and perspectives explained to me. I needed to have the why and how explained to me.

Eventually, I came to a profound wonder and apprecia-tion for the goodness of Vatican II. I can still recall the sense of gratitude that came to me as I read the proclamation in the Constitution on the Sacred Liturgy describing the liturgy as the work of all the faithful. This challenged the view of so many that somehow the liturgy is the work of the presider, in some ways set apart from the people. It became in many ways the foundation for our entire "new" vision of the Church as comprised of the total membership—clergy and laity together. In this document, the whole Church is called to "full, conscious, and active participation in liturgical celebrations" (*SC* 14). I believe that this summons is, in fact, the very foundation for the reemergence and growth of lay ministry that has occurred in the intervening years. For the first time, we came to appreciate a variety of roles in liturgy, and to understand that it was not only the ordained who exercised ministry and discharged offices in the liturgy. In article 29 we read: "Servers, readers, commentators, and members of the choir also exercise a genuine liturgical function. They ought, therefore, to discharge their offices with the sincere piety and decorum demanded by so exalted a ministry and rightly expected of them by God's people."

I was thrilled hearing the Church referred to as the People of God. I recognized the profound shift in the documents talking about the Church not as the hierarchy, but as the People of God. The mission of the Church is not given to the hierarchy but to the whole Church. Clergy and laity share in the one mission of God's people, and in the triple office of Jesus Christ as priest, prophet, and king. Development of the notion of collegiality only reinforced this appreciation of the Church as the entire People of God. In *Lumen Gentium*, bishops are no longer pictured as isolated monarchs but the emphasis is placed instead on the collective relationships among dioceses. In the years following the Council, collegiality became a benchmark for the shared ministries of all. In fact all these developments flowed from what has come to be understood by many as the most significant contribution of the Council, which is the Church's self-understanding as the People of God.

That shift in *Lumen Gentium* was a huge, unexpected breakthrough for me and for many. I wondered about what it meant that the Council participants had begun to talk about the Trinity as community and about its relationship to the

communion of saints. Intimately tied to both of these developments was the way baptism had begun to be presented. There
was now reference to the call and gifts of baptism, with new
application of these to *all* the baptized—with *all* the faithful
being called to holiness and empowerment.

I was aware even then that part of the implication of all
this was that the laity no longer had to wait for Father to call
for some sort of help or the support that he might need. Lay
people were called to become active in the Church, and the
ordained were now to call on them to coordinate and lead.
The hierarchy was being challenged to support *them* in their
ministry as the People of God!

Another major shift was the way the Council spoke of the
Church being engaged in the world, for God's own purposes.
That seemed absolutely wonderful to me. That Christians are
called to be succor, encouragement, help, and light to others—
that because of our faith we had wonderful things to share with
the world—was enormously encouraging to me. So was the
view that we need to live in the world, to be in conversation
with it, to be part of it. Until that point, there seemed to be a
sense that somehow we Catholics were to remain aloof from
the world and stand apart from those with whom we differed.
Practical examples of this sort of attitude are seen in the notion
that Catholics were not, except in rare circumstances, to enter
Protestant churches. And, if we did, we should not participate
in any way with the prayer of those communities. The strong
sense of boundaries surrounding the Church that I had known
as a boy was suddenly quite different.

In terms of implementing the Council and looking at
the implications of an ecclesiology based on the notion of the
Church as the People of God, I return to my earlier example
of we seminarians arriving at the North American College
in Rome from our home seminaries with different emphases
and different interests and areas of growth. That was true of

the dioceses of our country then and is certainly true today. It is not as if every diocese implemented the Council in the same way and at the same pace. Any observer can see that local Churches have responded differently to the promptings of the Spirit, to interpretations of the conciliar decrees and so forth. Some see things very simply: "The laws are there; what is the problem?" There are those who assume that every diocese should be exactly the same.

But we all face different problems at different times and in different ways. What do we do as a parish when our pastor is very old and too weak to preach on Sunday? Is it legitimate or not to call on someone who is trained and skillful at preaching to step forward to do that? Some say, "Yes, that's great. Of course, do it." Others insist that this may not be done. We know that the law is clear. But we know, too, that in the pastoral decisions of bishops, there is a genuine and legitimate leeway. Pastoral judgments have always taken precedence over an absolutely perfect outward compliance with the ecclesiastical laws in place at a given time. Sometimes, as we know, higher laws ought to prevail.

As we know, too, often enough there is no time to write down our reasons for these judgments. Full explanations are simply not possible. I believe we need to respond to the people who need our assistance. It is sometimes difficult to make time-constrained pastoral decisions that meet the legitimate needs of people and at the same time honor fully the relevant norms of the Church. Legal requirements, guidelines, and norms obviously do not all have the same weight and do not always apply in exactly the same way. Clearly, someone could take this to an extreme. But bishops simply are not doing that. I am not doing that. Perfect compliance is hardly the highest value. The sacraments are for the people. We celebrate them to help the Church be holy, not as an end in themselves. The Church is the People of God, in pilgrimage to more perfect union with our God. We absolutely have to signify this, signify what we honestly and really stand for. We have to keep our hearts where our treasure is.

Recall the story from Mark's gospel of the Lord's friends gathering bits of grain on the Sabbath. In so doing, they did not observe a particular law of Judaism. Even when challenged on their breaking of the law, Christ called his followers to do what they needed to do, insisting the Sabbath exists to serve the spiritual needs of people, not the other way around (Mk 2:23–28). These images live on in scripture and in the story of the Church because they help us to understand what the human condition is. We can't absolutize smaller things without diminishing our capacity to aspire to higher things. This is true for everyone, everywhere.

I have heard the adage "Keep the rule and rule will keep you." In my seminary years, a central switch turned off all the lights in the dormitories at the designated time. We probably learned discipline from that, and we learned that we couldn't act on our own preferences all the time. But circumstances change, and today the formation programs in seminaries are governed by different principles. Co-responsibility and respect-ful dialogue are much more the rules of operation today. In some ways, it's much easier to simply "follow the rules." There won't be many questions, and all will be clear and simple. But what do we risk in living that way?

My hope is that as we realize more and more what it is to be Church as the People of God, we will move toward a helpful diversity, always respecting the creedal formulae and dogmas, always striving for our deepest values, but recognizing that the living out of such values may find different expression in different times and places. We can be Church and still make decisions that differ—if these help us in achieving the deeper good for which we all strive.

In terms of considering future directions in the development of lay ecclesial ministry, I think we need to keep working on the issues identified in *Co-Workers in the Vineyard*. As I mentioned earlier, we need to be equitable and honest in the support we give to the development of lay ecclesial ministers. These people invest considerable time, energy, and money into their formation. They realize, as we do, that candidates for ordained ministry receive much fuller funding for their formation. This reality calls us to serious reflection on whether that situation should be preserved. It seems to me that we need to find concrete, practical ways to support all the people who are so willing to devote themselves to the pastoral ministry of the Church. It is our responsibility to do so.

We also need to keep working on the understanding of lay ecclesial ministry held by our communities at large. So many still equate ministry with that offered by the priest. That, of course, is appropriate as it relates to the sacraments that only a priest can administer. But I have met people who complain because they have not received ministry from a priest, even when a non-ordained minister has, in fact, come to them and cared for them beautifully. We need to help people understand that it is the ministry of Christ for which they thirst, and it is not the ordained alone who exercise that ministry and bring that service to us.

Progress in all these things will not be automatic by any means. I think it will come as all things do: through patient instruction and through careful, continuing reflection by both lay ministers and those to whom they offer ministry. We can respond in ways that promote understanding when there are complaints that Father should have come and not a lay person. Somehow we have to help one another realize Church as the People of God, too. To assume that "only Father" is good enough to exercise the ministry of Christ is surely not to appreciate this image.

As I think back on my youth, I realize that we equated all ministry with priestly ministry. We did not have at the time any real sense that our baptism incorporated us into a priestly people. The notion is deeply embedded in our tradition, but it did not become a vital, discussed reality in our lives until much later. When the Second Vatican Council re-enlivened that rich idea, it was a good example of how we come to appreciate our faith in new and deeper ways as history unfolds. We claim the same faith, but with more understanding and a different way of living and sharing it.

Today, we are blessed with thousands of lay ministers who extend the pastoral care of the Church in beautiful ways. When I was growing up in my hometown of Waterford, New York, our parish, St. Mary of the Assumption, was served faithfully and lovingly by the Augustinian Fathers of the Villanova Province. The priests were good to us, and we loved them.

But save for the lay catechists who taught us after school on Tuesday afternoons, we saw no other lay people in Church roles that we would now identify as ministerial. Those catechists, all women as I remember, were good to us. They treated us with respect and affection. And, although we kids didn't always behave as well as we should have, we had considerable respect and affection for them. We knew that they cared about us and sacrificed much for us. They were lay ministers long before anyone thought to call them that.

In the co-educational twelve hundred–student Catholic high school, which I attended, we were taught by priests, Sisters of Mercy, Sisters of Saint Joseph, and one lay person who taught music. At that time, we young people were aware that many women and men generously served the Church in volunteer and sometimes paid positions. But we were more likely to talk about their willingness to help Father than about their expressing their baptismal vocation through service to others. There was no developed theology of baptism as a sacrament of ministry, nor were there many opportunities for the ministerial enrichment and ongoing education of those lay persons. Now, of course, we see this kind of service as flowing from our baptism, as part of our obligation to share our gifts in service to the community, and in the building up of the Body of Christ for the transformation of the world.

What do I see down the road? I am optimistic about the future. In my view, the emergence of lay ecclesial ministry in the Church is not just a sign of innovation or revision but is a sign of true renewal and hope. I truly believe that it is a work of the Holy Spirit. There is much more to be done. We need to reflect continually on the experience of lay ecclesial ministers and on our experience of their ministry. We need to work on the areas outlined in *Co-Workers in the Vineyard*: recruitment, initial and on-going support, relationships with bishops and other ministers of the Gospel, relationships with the people they serve, compensation, and accountability.

If we can do this work in faith and with mutual respect— and I have no doubt that we can—we can be an integral part of the continued growth of one of God's greatest gifts to the post-conciliar Church.

2

What Lay Ecclesial Ministers Say

I would be remiss if I did not include in this book the voices of the lay ecclesial ministers about whom I write, at least those with whom I have experience in the Diocese of Rochester. I have included several of their personal essays in this book as a way to amplify what I see as the general perceptions I have encountered.

In recent months, as I gathered my thoughts for writing this book, I have sat with many lay ecclesial ministers in open, spirited, and refreshingly honest conversations. They speak freely about how they perceive their roles, the sources from which they draw their strength, and the problems and tensions of their ministries. They speak equally freely about the moments of pure joy that they experience daily and about the way they think others perceive them. I will let them speak freely here as well, for to ignore their real and heartfelt thoughts would be to ignore the questions that will further the Church's work of sorting out this "new thing." Their thoughts and observations very much reveal the issues the Church faces as lay ecclesial ministry expands and evolves.

I imagine the conversations in other dioceses would run along similar lines, but certainly here in our diocese lay ecclesial ministers are fully aware that their roles are still being defined by the very Church that has called forth their gifts. They know full well that their work is sometimes in tension—or at least perceived to be in tension—with that of the ordained, and that the people in the pews both appreciate and still misunderstand their work and their role in the Church.

The majority of lay ministers with whom I spoke are graduates of our diocese's St. Bernard's School of Theology and Ministry, so a little background on St. Bernard's seems in order. In response to the Second Vatican Council, St. Bernard's Seminary changed rapidly and became one of the first Roman Catholic seminaries in the United States to open its doors to laity.

On June 30, 1981, St. Bernard's Seminary officially closed its four-year program of priestly formation and moved from its long-time facilities. All other academic programs were transferred to St. Bernard's Institute. The focus on ministerial and theological education for the laity intensified with the move from the north side of Rochester to the Colgate Rochester Divinity School campus in the city of Rochester. On August 26 of that same year, St. Bernard's and the Colgate Rochester Divinity School—a nationally known Baptist seminary— signed a covenant establishing a graduate-level affiliation between the two institutions. Under this arrangement, both institutions would retain their own curricula, degrees, endowments, alumni, and boards of trustees. Both institutions would share the physical facilities of what is now the Colgate Rochester Crozer Divinity School campus, maintaining a single library, and, within curriculum requirements, extended cross-registration privileges to all enrolled students.

In the fall of 1989, St. Bernard's initiated an extension program in the Diocese of Albany with the enthusiastic support of Bishop Howard Hubbard. St. Bernard's program at Albany serves the educational and ministerial needs of the Roman Catholic Diocese of Albany, as well as the wider ecumenical community of the region.

In the spring of 1992, the Diocese of Rochester started a non-graduate training program for people serving in and preparing for parish ministry. This program, known as the Certification Program, continues to serve as the diocesan training program for many parish leaders while also providing opportunities for individuals seeking adult faith formation. A comparable program known as the *Instituto de Pastoral Hispano* is offered for the Hispanic community.

In the fall of 1994, the Certification for Designated Ministry program, the Instituto de Pastoral Hispano, and the Office of Professional Development were incorporated into the structure of St. Bernard's. The consolidation of these educational programs with the graduate program brings both better collaboration and clarity to the diverse levels of preparation for ministry. The integration of the Certification and Community Education programs into the overall mission of St. Bernard's signaled the emerging role of the school as the ministerial training center for the Diocese of Rochester. In 2002, the Certification program was extended to the Albany Diocese, further enhancing St. Bernard's role in preparing a wider range of people for ministry.

In August 2003, St. Bernard's moved to a brand new facility in suburban Rochester. This marks an exciting new phase in the history of the school, which has a vibrant educational and ministerial formation program for those seeking lives in professional ministry both ordained and lay.

One resounding message from these good people is that their ministry "is not just a job. It's a call." Indeed, the many lay ecclesial ministers with whom I spoke consider their service to the Church as a direct call from God, a movement of the

Holy Spirit in their lives and in the Church's movement and growth. *Co-Workers in The Vineyard of the Lord* documents similar themes and defines this tug of God to serve the Church as a lay ecclesial minister "a special grace."

> Lay ecclesial ministers are members of the lay faithful, sharing in the common priesthood of all the baptized. As such, they are called to discipleship and "to illuminate and order all temporal things with which they are closely associated that these may always be affected and grow according to Christ" (*LG*, 31).
>
> The further call of some persons to lay ecclesial ministry adds a special grace by which the Holy Spirit "makes them fit and ready to undertake various tasks and offices for the renewal and building up of the Church" (*LG*, 12). Lay ecclesial ministry flows from an explicit faith commitment and is animated by the love of God and neighbor. It also entails an explicit relationship of mutual accountability to and collaboration with the Church hierarchy.
>
> —*Co-Workers in the Vineyard of the Lord*, p. 25

In our own diocese, lay ecclesial ministers speak humbly but confidently about this call. "I feel I have been called forth to do a special work," one woman said. Another added, "The calling comes in pieces. First, you discover your calling. Next, there is a process of discernment. Then at some point you get the affirmation of the Church and feedback from the community, the People of God. It is much more than a job. There is a spiritual strength that allows me to be fed, to feed, to be fulfilled and to fulfill."

This sense of call is important because by understanding their work to be divinely inspired and driven and by fulfilling the many requirements of preparation we ask of them, many lay ecclesial ministers naturally feel their ministry is distinctive, more clearly defined, and more professional than that of their peers in the pews. "It's more than *volunteer* work in Church," one woman said to nods of affirmation from her fellow ministers.

I am reminded here of a fellow bishop who worried aloud to me not long ago that somehow we have created a new class in the Church with this new title of lay ecclesial minister. But I do not sense among the vast majority of these ministers with whom I have conversed any overt sense of entitlement or privilege or feeling of being set apart. Although the distinction itself, as we have seen, has created the need to sort out new issues and trod new paths to understanding.

What I do sense from these ministers is a strong confidence in their roles, a sense of mission that gives them a willingness to tackle most any obstacle. This confidence is bolstered by a conviction that their work—and the considerable sacrifice they make in using their gifts for the benefit of the Church and not in higher-paying corporate employment—is indeed divinely inspired.

Despite what I feel is an overwhelmingly positive experience and acceptance in the Diocese of Rochester, lay ministers do perceive that obstacles are needlessly placed in their way. For some, there is a perception that their work is not fully respected by the Church hierarchy or by the faithful. Some lay ecclesial ministers, especially those called according to Canon 517 §2 to lead parishes as pastoral administrators—the title we give them in our diocese—feel a little like the characters in the hit movie of some years back called *The Replacements*. In that film, a group of amateur football players is hired to fill out the ranks of a striking professional football team. Although the team of replacements is eventually victorious, they know in the beginning that they are second-class, merely a convenient solution by the team owners to keep the franchise alive. Some, perhaps many, lay ecclesial ministers feel the same about their positions in the Church. Many fear at least at times that their fellow Catholics perceive them as little more than replacements until the *real* ministers show up.

One lay ecclesial minister told me, "My belief is that I have received a call by virtue of my own charisms and giftedness, rather than, 'I'm doing this for Father.'" Others echo her thoughts: "Some people appreciate lay leadership, but others don't. They want a priest." I also hear, "If Father doesn't say it, it hasn't been said."

More than one pastoral administrator has been surprised to receive, from a diocesan office, a form letter beginning "Dear Father." Anecdotes of this type abound at ministerial gatherings, most of them incidental or accidental. Taken together, however, they can undermine the morale of the very people the Church needs so desperately.

"I was taken aback," a female pastoral administrator for one of our suburban Rochester parishes said, "by noticing that the Kenedy Directory [the official national Catholic directory], which used to list the pastoral administrator first, now lists the sacramental minister first—because he is a priest. It's not big, but symbolically it points to one aspect of diminishment."

Others long for more authority, such as the man who indicated to our discussion group that he could do so much more if allowed by the Church to do so. "I'm capable, trained, and spiritually alive enough in a Church that is hungry for my ministry," he said. "But in certain circumstances, my hands are 'officially' tied."

This frustration is perhaps nowhere more evident than in the area of preaching. It is widely noticed that many lay ecclesial ministers have gifts for preaching and teaching and that these are grounded in a theological base that is current, orthodox, and engaging. Some churchgoers who say they are insulted by the poor homilies given by some priests are baffled that the lay minister is not permitted to preach except under stringently defined circumstances. Of course, there are other churchgoers who want only priests to preach, no matter what the circumstances.

On the flip side, some lay ecclesial ministers themselves acknowledge their worries that their presence has become so strong—more than thirty thousand nationally—that this is already diluting the role reserved for the ordained and the sacramental life of the Catholic Church.

"Sometimes I have mixed emotions about my own leadership and expertise," said one lay ecclesial minister. "I have to say that one danger we face is losing the sense of an essential aspect of our Church—and that is the sacramental priesthood. Even while people at the nursing home are very welcoming to me and affirm my gifts and ministry, they still never encounter a priest. So I've developed a real sense that the sacramental priesthood could be losing its importance in the community."

My conversations with actual lay ministers, as I prepared to write this book, have left me with an awareness of the richness that this new development and those most directly involved with it bring to the Church. I witnessed deep joy in the presence and testimony of those with whom I met. I heard descriptions of the way ministry has become the very foundation and context for so many of these ministers' relationships with God. I also learned how so many experience their ministries not as "Church jobs" but as calls from and responses to God acting in their lives. I am deeply impressed by the way these women and men exercise such great care and responsibility for their work, by their competence and professionalism, and by the deep compassion I saw in so many.

Having said all that, I also witnessed through them some of the more negative effects that the questions and difficulties surrounding lay ministry can have. There is a real lack of job security in many of the positions open to lay ecclesial ministers, and the loss of a job, as we know, has deep and harmful effects on families. A new pastor, for example, can mean the end of a fruitful ministry in some cases. Misunderstanding and resentment—even from those being served—can be hurtful, especially when a sense of being perceived as second-rate or only a stand-in for an ordained minister is conveyed.

Questions about liturgical roles and leadership in ministry contribute to considerable tension and disharmony, as they have for many years. I appreciated very much learning of some unease among these lay ecclesial ministers who are concerned that a lack of contact with priests is contributing to a deficient understanding of that ministry among some Catholics. That observation took me somewhat by surprise, as I had not been aware of it prior to these sessions.

3

Voices from the Vineyard:
Rose Davis

I love being a pastoral minister. And I love being a wife. And I love being a mother. In a similar way, I feel "made for" each of these vocations. They are not jobs. They are who I am. They fit.

I didn't grow up dreaming of being a wife, mother, or pastoral minister. The process of becoming a wife and mother was, for me, an experience of life, and of God's plan, unfolding one unexpected step at a time. In retrospect, I see a pattern of my responses to what seemed like God's isolated suggestions. God's nudges, and my responses, led me to a life as wife and mother that continues to surprise and delight me. This life satisfies, challenges, and uses every good thing I have to offer for the sake of those I love.

My journey to pastoral ministry unfolded similarly: increasing attraction to the sacramental life of the Church; the urge to help others find the hope in Christ that I find; a desire to know more about my Catholic faith; responses to God's promptings that I volunteer in my parish and pursue theological education; even the profound awareness that, in being wife and mother, I had been taught how to stretch in order to love others. In retrospect all these things were God leading me to full-time lay ecclesial ministry. This, too, is a life and a calling that delights, satisfies, and challenges me—and uses me up.

In the early 1990s, having volunteered in various parish ministries and having completed a master's degree in theology, I felt a strong pull toward pursuing full-time parish ministry. But I also struggled to discern the proper expression of my response to God's clear call. As a lifelong Roman Catholic, my memory was filled with images of priests in all kinds of ministry, doing the kinds of work that I, too, felt called to do. It was confusing and sometimes a little scary. I wanted to be respectful, and yet I tried not to be afraid or overly reluctant.

I began to work as a pastoral associate in a small urban parish with one assigned priest, a pastor, in his sixties. The pastor and I began our new positions at the same time. He and I found it easy to talk with one another about our faith in Christ and about our love for the Church and for ministry. That was a great gift. He appreciated the care I tried to take in determining which work belonged to him as an ordained person and which was more appropriately mine as lay minister. But he also challenged me to minister beyond my comfort zone.

Over time, my pastor asked me to take on various responsibilities not reserved for a priest, though often I provided ministry that people had come to expect from a priest. This new approach stretched the pastor, me, and the parish we served. I appreciated that the pastor conscientiously helped parishioners understand my role. And he told me that he appreciated the times when I challenged him, sometimes saying to him, "Thanks for your confidence in me here, but I think this is where they need you, their priest." A model of ministry emerged in that parish in a very natural way. It was a model that respected the role of both ordained and lay ecclesial ministers.

As I worked, two experiences affirmed my call to ministry. First was the simple realization that the one priest assigned to the parish could not fulfill the pastoral needs of parishioners and neighbors all by himself. Without my help, people would "go without," or this pastor's health might be compromised. He did not shy away from hard work and made himself constantly available to parishioners, but he could not do everything. The second affirmation was more personal. It was the experience of people telling me that, through my parish work, *I* had helped them on their journey of faith. They pointed to something about my gender or my personality, or about my experience as married person or parent, that had allowed *my ministry* to them to be a particular bridge to Christ and to the Catholic Church.

In a way that surprised me at first, I have experienced ministry to be very much like parenting. But doesn't that really make sense? Both vocations have the same fundamental goal: to love the people God has placed in your care and help them attain the fullness of life that God intends for them. Perhaps this is the Church's insight when it calls the family "the domestic Church." In human families, the roles of parents are not necessarily competitive; rather, they are unique and complementary. Single parents may beautifully, and valiantly, struggle to raise their families, but as a society, we recognize that two good parents create synergy. They offer one another support and possess varied gifts and characteristics, and their interrelationship, exchange of ideas, and communion of love enrich the family.

It seems to me that this God-designed parenting model could be helpful in thinking about the future of our hierarchical Church. I have been blessed to work with wonderful, collaborative pastors who have been open to new models and have valued the complementarities of men and women, lay and ordained. I have experienced the synergy of this collaboration and the new life it inspires in a parish. The Catholic Church I love, and hope for, and look forward to, is one in which lay ecclesial ministers, those lay persons who answer God's call to devote their lives to service in the Church, will be welcomed not as support staff, but as full partners in Catholic pastoral ministry.

4

A Consideration of History

As we look back at early Christianity, we do so from the perspective of our own time and place. We might assume that the best way to interpret ministry as it existed in the early Church is to compare and contrast the two primary models of ministry that we see operative in the Church today, namely ordained and lay. For example, we may want to ask: What ministries were open to lay people in the first years of Christianity? Which ones were restricted to the ordained? Were particular ministries assumed by certain stable groups or communities of early Christians?

These questions of course take account of *our* experience very well, but they don't reflect the realities of the early Christian centuries. From the sources of early Christianity, and from those whose life's work has been to study and understand these writings, we learn that the emergence of ministries in the early Church was a complex and varied process, differing from region to region and across time. I will briefly outline some of the major developments in the evolution of ministry, hoping to provide a context that will help us appreciate the roots of the ministry patterns we witness in our own time.

As I understand it, "ministries" in the first centuries of Christianity were simply not structured in the ways we have witnessed in our own time. Moreover, there was no uniform blueprint to be followed as new ministries emerged. The reality was that the various churches did not structure their practices in identical ways. We know that the churches in Rome, North Africa, Egypt, and Asia Minor developed quite distinctively in terms of the ways new ministries emerged, were recognized, and were incorporated into the lives of those communities.

Historians of Christianity testify to the fact that it would simply make no sense to imagine the existence of a large group of lay Christians living an almost passive religious existence while a second distinct group of ordained clerics were charged with the recognizable Church jobs of presiding at liturgy, pastoral care, institutional decision making, and policy formation.

Rather, the process of shaping the early Church moved from its original focus on the life and ministry of Jesus to relying on and recognizing the varied gifts—or charisms—of those who became part of the community that rose around him. In many places the offices taken over from the synagogue provided basic church structures. In the first two centuries, at least, there was not a distinction between ordained and lay. From this initial and very loose structure, more formal patterns of ministry began to emerge across all the early church communities. But the patterns certainly did not develop in uniform ways.

Thus a whole range of tasks and functions associated with early ministries are mentioned in the New Testament: preaching, healing, discerning, teaching, giving aid to those in need, and so forth. While several different lists of ministries are provided in the New Testament (see, for example, 1 Corinthians 12:8–10, 1 Corinthians 12:28, Romans 12:7–8, and Ephesians 4:11), there seems never to have been a sense that a closed or final list would be desired, expected, or forthcoming in the near future. What these functions apparently had in common were their rootedness in the Spirit and their link with baptism, as exemplified in the following much-loved passage from 1 Corinthians.

> There are different kinds of spiritual gifts but the same Spirit;
> there are different forms of service but the same Lord;
> there are different workings but the same God who produces all of them in everyone.
> To each individual the manifestation of the Spirit is given for some benefit.
> To one is given through the Spirit the expression of wisdom; to another the expression of knowledge according to the same Spirit;
> to another faith by the same Spirit; to another gifts of healing by the one Spirit;
> to another mighty deeds; to another prophecy; to another discernment of spirits; to another varieties of tongues; to another interpretation of tongues.
> But one and the same Spirit produces all of these, distributing them individually to each person as he wishes.
> As a body is one though it has many parts, and all the parts of the body, though many, are one body, so also Christ.
> For in one Spirit we were all baptized into one body, whether Jews or Greeks, slaves or free persons, and we were all given to drink of one Spirit.
> —1 Corinthians 12:4–13

These ministries were also similar in their intention to provide a form of service that would sustain and build up the community.

> And he gave some as apostles, others as prophets,
> others as evangelists, others as pastors and teachers,
> to equip the holy ones for the work of ministry, for
> building up the body of Christ, until we all attain
> to the unity of faith and knowledge of the Son of
> God, to maturity, to the extent of the full stature
> of Christ.
>
> —Ephesians 4:11–13

Lastly, these earliest Christian ministries seem to have shared a propensity for occasional disputes that proved difficult to regulate or control. (Read, for example, the accounts of 1 Corinthians 14, 2 Thessalonians 2:1–15, and 2 Peter 3:1–16).

In every individual church during this period, what prevailed was a spirit of responding to needs as they emerged. Permanent "states of life" determining which form of service would be rendered by an individual had not yet solidified, and ordination, at least as we know it, did not exist. Moreover, the ministries that emerged were very much tied to the particular community and its needs, providing a way of supplying the services and coordinating the functions that were necessary for sustaining the life and work of the group at hand.

While the work of the Spirit and reliance on the gifts of the Spirit (charisma) were primary, we find in the New Testament references to suggest that some initial structuring of ministerial functions was already beginning to emerge. Thus we discover in passages referring to the twelve, the words "apostle" and "presbyter." We also read about deacons, prophets, teachers, and leaders in various places. We are provided glimpses of situations in individual churches that appear quite different, one from the other. Corinth, for example, apparently relied particularly on the charismatic ministries, while Philippi recognized bishops and deacons. Prophets and teachers served the community at Antioch; presbyters and elders came to be significant there; and 1 and 2 Timothy and Titus mention even more defined ministries, perhaps reminiscent of the closer associations of those communities with the detailed, well-defined structures of Jewish life, particularly Mosaic Law.

This very early phenomenon of a largely decentralized and eclectic pattern of emerging ministries during the first two centuries of the Christian era underwent significant modification in the centuries that followed. Many of these changes were the direct result of the Church adapting to fit structures similar to those prevailing in the surrounding political world of the time. Some other changes seem to have depended on a response to conflict within the Church itself. Still others arose as the Church tried to respond to threats from outside.

By recognizing and exploring how these various developments affected the way ministry came to be understood and carried out, we can better understand the patterns that have dominated our own experiences of Church ministry in recent decades. This will also help to provide a context for the changes we are now witnessing in that model.

I see four developments as particularly influential in laying the foundation for the ministry patterns that prevailed in Catholic consciousness in the United States through most of the twentieth century. The re-emergence of lay ecclesial ministry in our own time is primarily rooted in developments leading up to, and emerging from, the Second Vatican Council. This re-emergence continues to take place in a context dominated by these very patterns and to some degree must be understood over and against them.

1. Church authority and governance become linked with the office of bishop and the ordines.

Emerging structures and patterns of ministry in the post–New Testament Church often relied very directly on parallels taken from the surrounding Roman culture and government. Just as the organization of civic life at the time depended on the exercise of authority by a central, pivotal person holding an established office with clearly delineated powers, so the office of bishop grew increasingly pivotal for the life of the Christian community. We know that Roman law was a highly respected and useful tool of government, and the general scheme was that it established a "class" or group of rulers who were charged with civic administration, a pattern that developed throughout the Roman Empire.

As the Church set about the task of structuring itself for governance and order, we can detect this same pattern taking hold. This can be seen in the writings of Ignatius of Antioch and Cyprian of Carthage as clearly as anywhere. Along with the emergence of a dominant and influential office of bishop, the Church of Carthage adapted a parallel to the Roman bench, or *ordo*, which was originally a structure of senators and army commanders charged with civil governance. The individual bishops of Africa, for example, eventually came together as a kind of ecclesiastical *ordo,* or council, to oversee ecclesial life in their jurisdiction. The parallel with secular governance structures is undeniable.

At any rate, this adaptation to the structures of secular government affected the ways in which ministry came to be exercised over the next centuries of the Church. Historians point out that throughout the Constantinian era (early fourth century) and beyond, bishops were no longer chosen by the people, as had been the practice in earlier centuries. They often came to be appointed by secular officials. Centuries later, a more centralized Church would control the appointment of bishops entirely. As the choosing of bishops was removed from the laity, a separation between the office of bishop and the laity became clearer. This shift also demonstrates a diminishment in the influence and power of the laity in the administration of the Church.

As was the parallel with civil government, a governing class emerged within the Church. The clergy provided a kind of ruling caste for the masses of Christians. It is likely that this type of structure appealed to most Church members at the time, since it was what they were experiencing in the culture around them. As Church organization became more closely aligned with Roman regional districts, bishops assumed singular exercise of Church authority, coming eventually to share these powers with the priests, or presbyters. Thus, Church governance came to be exercised solely by those who were ordained. In fact, the Church came to be more and more associated with the ordained hierarchy, or those with ministerial and administrative authority.

2. Ordination becomes a separate state of life, and ministry is equated with it.

As we have seen, the fact that Cyprian (d. 258) actually instituted an *ordo* or order of ruling bishops, modeled after secular officialdom in Carthage, is not surprising in the sense that the world of secular governance used that very structure. It did mean, however, that the ordained—bishops, presbyters, and deacons—eventually came to constitute a separate group set apart from and distinguished from the laity. Ministry came to be seen as the function of the smaller group of the ordained, while the function of the laity was more akin to the ordinary citizenry of the Roman Empire, accustomed to being governed by a designated group set apart and established as the ruling order.

Thus, in any sense in which we know it today, ministry was gradually restricted to those in orders, whose roles extended to teaching, preaching, witnessing marriages, absolving sins, presiding at liturgy, and so forth. Gradually, lay persons were formally and legislatively excluded from holding office in the governance of the Church.

The distinction between clergy and laity was reinforced in other ways as well. Cyprian and others adopted the secular practice of excluding women from the ruling structures. Tertullian, Cyprian's mentor, wrote: "A woman is not permitted to speak in the Church, nor yet to teach, nor baptize, nor offer, nor yet claim to herself the right of any masculine function, much less of the sacerdotal office." The place of all laity was apparently diminishing in these years, but women were explicitly identified in a number of passages as unfit for assisting in the work of the Church.

The more biblical notion of the priesthood of believers seems still to have been an accepted tenet at the time, but the emergence of the ruling class of the ministerial priesthood was gradually becoming the norm not only in terms of Church administration and order, but in terms of legislation pertaining to worship as well. Tertullian wrote, "Where there is no Bench of ecclesiastical order you [a lay man] offer [the sacrifice] and you baptize and are your own sole priest." Obviously, a distinction between those in "ecclesiastical order" and the laity was becoming more and more pronounced, even as early as the third century. Ministry was gradually concentrated into a range of functions, all of which were properly exercised by the ordained.

3. Celibacy is gradually adopted, eventually being legislated for those ordained.

These developments in Church governance and the structure of worship took place as another trend also unfolded that would affect the exercise and experience of ministry. It was the gradual acceptance of celibacy as inherent to the priesthood. We see mention of this on an official level as early as the Council of Elvira in 305, even though celibacy was not finally and formally legislated for the western Church until the First and Second Lateran Councils in 1123 and 1139, respectively.

No single factor led to the emergence of celibacy as a requirement for the ordained priesthood in the west. Rather, a variety of factors contributed to this development, some more philosophical and theological, some having to do with reform efforts in the face of various kinds of corruption.

One example is the growth of a dualistic anthropology in which the soul and the spiritual powers of the human person were almost opposed to the body, and even to human emotions. This tendency combined with a suspicion of human passion and feeling that was associated with stoicism. Monasticism, originally a lay movement, gradually replaced martyrdom as the pinnacle of holiness in a post-persecution Church. As this shift unfolded, the expectation of celibacy began to be imposed upon clerics.

Meanwhile, the dominant Christological thought through much of the history of the Church, very much emphasized the divinity, not the humanity, of Jesus Christ. Priests, referred to oftentimes as "other Christs," were naturally viewed in this light. As the Old Testament became a more prominent reference point for the rites of the Eucharist, the practice of requiring abstinence from sex before offering the holy sacrifice took root. This practice grew out of the Old Testament accounts of priestly requirements surrounding the offering of Temple sacrifices. As this practice of abstaining from sex became more and more ingrained, it became associated with the whole of priestly life. Eventually, celibacy came to be initially the preferred, and later on the legislated, state of those who would preside at the Eucharistic celebration. It would, thus, become the required state of life for those in ministry.

Over the centuries, there eventually emerged an entirely separate clerical state of life, whose members lived a lifestyle very different from most of the Church. This could not help but reinforce an increasingly rigid separation between the majority of Christians and the clergy. The fact that ministry came to be associated with the ordained or those in religious orders helped to solidify the notion that ministry was simply not the domain of the laity. This was true whether ministry was directed toward care for the community or service with or to the "outside" world. Various pronouncements of the Church reinforced this notion, and the contrast with what now seems clear to have been New Testament evidence of a far more broadly reaching practice of ministry seems not to have been noticed or attended to at the time.

4. The secular and the sacred are gradually distinguished one from the other, with unfortunate implications for the understanding and practice of ministry.

By the beginning of the second millennium there are well-documented sources citing the widely held view that Christian society had two ends: one spiritual, one material. This worldview readily gave rise to a distinction in power and responsibility between the civil order and the Church. Emperors, governors, kings, and the like held secular authority, while bishops and priests controlled the spiritual realm.

The Bishop of Rome, by now a very pronounced office and a parallel center of power to the secular regime, would hold responsibility for spiritual matters. Naturally, the spiritual end was the higher, so the pope and religious authorities gained a degree of supremacy through this philosophical schema. The spiritual power held by the pope was shared with other bishops, and in turn with priests and deacons. In the reforms associated with Pope Gregory VII in the eleventh century and articulated through a host of documents and other writings, bishops and priests were responsible for the spiritual domain, while secular powers controlled temporal affairs.

As this dualism became more prominent, ministry was more and more associated with the inner life of the Church. It was, as we have seen already, increasingly limited to the ordained clergy, now understood as an almost sacred caste, clearly set apart from the rest of Christians. Laity, those not ordained or in religious orders and thus not in this special caste, came gradually to assume what would be their appropriate role in this scheme. The proper arena for the activities of the laity was in the secular order—out in the world, not within the Church.

As we look back on these developments from our own vantage point of the twenty-first century, we see how very natural and incremental shifts came to have much larger implications for ministry. These shifts became theologically significant not only in separating the work of the laity from that of the clergy, but also in contributing to the emergence of a spirituality that stressed a separation between the Christian's ordinary life and his or her spiritual life.

We know that centuries later the Second Vatican Council actually had to include a chapter in *Lumen Gentium* entitled "The Universal Call to Holiness," hoping to bridge the chasm between ordinary life and the Gospel, between the "spiritual" work of the hierarchy and the "secular" work of laity. Holiness was reclaimed as a call and gift to *all* Christians, and this along with many other fruits of Vatican II has profoundly changed our modern view of the role of the laity and of any discussion of the role of lay ecclesial ministry. In May 2009, Pope Benedict XVI reminded participants at a conference in the Diocese of Rome called "Church Membership and Pastoral Co-responsibility" that we still have a long way to go in understanding and assuming our rightful obligations as persons baptized into Christ. He called for a "change of mentality" and said, "There should be a renewed becoming aware of our being Church and of the pastoral co-responsibility that, in the name of Christ, all of us are called to carry out."

5

Voices from the Vineyard: Patrick Fox

As a "twenty-something" person with four years of teaching experience and a degree in theology, I came to my first parish experience in 1972. I was hired as the coordinator of religious education *and* supervisor of maintenance. Among the requests that first year: to teach boys to use the bathrooms without missing the mark and to wash Pastor's car. It was an inauspicious beginning to what has been a life of joy in service to the Church and a great opportunity to learn about people, faith, and the art of joining the mission to which Jesus invites us.

Since that time, I have served in five parishes and two schools and on a diocesan staff. Each community has taught me much about the goodness of the People of God and allowed me to serve—warts and all—with many others at the service of all God's people.

Today we are using the terminology "lay ecclesial ministers." I have been known by titles of coordinator, director, team leader, and others, and the best lesson I have learned is this: I know I am supposed to be in charge but question if I am, or should even try to be, in control. When all is said and done, I know that I am not in control or in charge. I have made the greatest mess when I have assumed the latter and been frustrated at the former.

What I have learned along the way is that I am the student. I have been enriched and am able to rise to stewardship of the gifts God has granted me when I have allowed myself to be mentored by the youth I have been privileged to serve, and mentored by the adults who have been stewards of this faith longer than I. In this, I trust that some good has been accomplished.

My ministerial journey was born when I was encouraged to consider priesthood, a role to which I freely admit I never felt called. I spent six years in a community of men who served in educational ministry and to whom I remain indebted for helping me focus my call and gain both a rooted spirituality and a level of confidence that enabled me to enter lay ministry. This lay ministry I have known for almost forty years, where the default perception was so often—in the early days at least—that one landed "here" because they were unable to make it "there."

The truth is I chose "here." With the grace of God and the help of many people I trust I have been of some service.

I say that because, as I look back, I see what I would offer to those just beginning. I would say to them that when day is done, for all its warts (just like mine) this Church is as strong or weak as each person. Some of those weak and strong people are called to be lay ecclesial ministers. My sense is that if we respond to the call of the Spirit with sincere and humble hearts we are God's Chosen People. God will use our gifts, give us the grace of the Spirit, and allow us to be fed by others on the journey we call ministry.

6

The Impact of Vatican II

I t is impossible to overestimate the effect of the Second Vatican Council (1962–1965) on lay ecclesial ministry. If the centuries of the first two millennia of the Christian era were marked by a gradual narrowing of ministry and an enduring diminishment of the role of the laity in the Church, Vatican II brought an abrupt reversal to both trends. The decrees of the Council themselves, and the speeches and decisions that led to adoption of the documents in their final form, combine to provide the image of a Church passionately searching for ways to address the many challenges that came from both cultural and theological sources in the intervening years since the First Vatican Council (1869–1870). Almost every innovation by the Council would eventually have an impact on the way in which the role of the laity came to be perceived and would affect in quite particular ways the rapid growth of lay ecclesial ministry.

For our purposes, I will focus on six major theological directions established by *Lumen Gentium*.

1. Church as the "People of God" and Trajectories of *Lumen Gentium*

2. Retrieval of the Biblical Notion of Charism
3. A Return to *Diakonia* or Servant Leadership
4. The Priestly, Prophetic, and Kingly Ministry of the Whole People of God
5. The Universal Call to Holiness
6. Recovering the Permanent Diaconate

These are already well documented, but I will highlight ways in which *Lumen Gentium* altered understandings that had surrounded ministry in the years preceding the Council, thus providing the possibility of new ecclesial pathways into the future.

1. Church as the "People of God" and Trajectories of Lumen Gentium

I will begin by citing what is for me the most obvious and still the most significant shift introduced by *Lumen Gentium*. This is the change in the final order of the chapters of the document. The chapter on the "People of God" was, in the end, placed ahead of the chapter on the hierarchical structure of the Church. This well documented and, at the time, highly controversial and unexpected shift from the originally planned outline carried a number of significant theological implications. None was more important than the establishment of a single identity for both ordained and lay Catholics as the People of God.

After centuries of identifying the ministries of the Church with those in orders, this single move provided a wider context that would include both clergy and laity. Together, we are *all* the People of God. Rather than depict an almost "bi-level" church with clergy ranking over the laity, the People of God identification would now reinforce the common identity and sacred unity of the whole Catholic Church. Whatever ministry was exercised, whatever service would be offered, whatever ecclesial standing one undertook, every function would exist for the building up of the single community of the Church, which is constituted by all of us.

The People of God became a major theme of the whole Council. It came to provide the context for identifying the Church's understanding of itself, which could no longer be identified exclusively with the hierarchy. From this point onward, the Church would realize itself overtly and self-consciously as the gathering of all the baptized. In fact, the ministry of the hierarchy was not defined as an end in itself, but was now beginning to be seen anew as directed toward facilitating the ministry of all the baptized.

Within this context of a general revision in the self-understanding of the Church, several passages explicitly address the reality of lay ministry. In *Apostolicam Actuositatem*, the Decree on the Apostolate of the Laity (*AA*), the hierarchy's support for the lay apostolate is explicit, when the Council states:

> Finally, the hierarchy entrusts to the laity certain functions which are more closely connected with pastoral duties, such as the teaching of Christian doctrine, certain liturgical actions, and the care of souls. By virtue of this mission, the laity are fully subject to higher ecclesiastical control in the performance of this work (24).

And again in *Lumen Gentium*:

> Besides this apostolate which certainly pertains to all Christians, the laity can also be called in various ways to a more direct form of cooperation in the apostolate of the Hierarchy. This was the way certain men and women assisted Paul the Apostle in the Gospel, laboring much in the Lord. Further, they have the capacity to assume from the

Hierarchy certain ecclesiastical functions, which are to be performed for a spiritual purpose (33).

2. Retrieval of the Biblical Notion of Charism

A second development affecting lay ministry was the Council's retrieval of the biblical theology of charisms, or gifts extended to all the baptized by the Spirit. This theology challenged centuries of associating ministry with a particular state of life that provided elevated status within the Church. This theology of charism returned our understanding to a more biblical and *functional* understanding of the origins and sources of ministry. Whatever function was undertaken on behalf of the Gospel would be for the building up of the community, rooted in baptism, and inspired by the Holy Spirit.

If common understandings would have situated the foundation for ministry with office in the Church, several passages from *Lumen Gentium* clearly suggest otherwise. In speaking about the three-fold ministry of Christ extended to all, the document moves in the direction of establishing charism, not office, as the foundation for all ministry.

> Allotting his gifts according as he wills (cf. 1 Cor 12:11), he also distributes special graces among the faithful of every rank. By these gifts he makes them fit and ready to undertake various tasks and offices for the renewal and building up of the Church, as it is written, "the manifestation of the Spirit is given to everyone for profit" (1 Cor 12:7). Whether these charisms be very remarkable or more simple and widely diffused, they are to be received with thanksgiving and consolation since they are fitting and useful for the needs of the Church.
>
> —*Lumen Gentium,* 12

In this passage, charism is not viewed as an extraordinary gift for extraordinary times, but as the work of the Spirit bestowed upon all for the building up of the Church. Any notion of a divide between those exercising ministry and those receiving it is diminished with the common foundation of all "tasks and offices."

3. A Return to Diakonia or Servant Leadership

A third shift involved recalling the strong, rich, biblical notion of *diakonia,* or service. Actions undertaken through ministry were to be rooted in and directed toward service. By recognizing the foundation of ministry as service to the community, the Council opened the door for the "variety of ministries" intended for the building up of the whole People of God.

> For the nurturing and constant growth of the People of God, Christ the Lord instituted in His Church a variety of ministries, which work for the good of the whole body. For those ministers, who are endowed with sacred power, serve their brethren, so that all who are of the People of God, and therefore enjoy a true Christian dignity, working toward a common goal freely and in an orderly way, may arrive at salvation.
>
> —*Lumen Gentium*, 18

It also ended a centuries-long pattern of associating ministry with a "caste" or "bench," which meant, by practical extension, that ministry not only came to be exclusively associated with the ordained but to be seen as the source of a privileged, autonomous authority over those not ordained.

4. The Priestly, Prophetic, and Kingly Ministry of the Whole People of God

A fourth and highly significant move arose from the application of the three-fold ministry of Christ to all the baptized rather than to the hierarchy alone. The priestly, prophetic, and kingly dimensions of the ministry of Christ are now associated with the sacrament of baptism and only secondarily with the sacrament of orders. This association dramatically altered the perception that the ministry of the laity was properly directed to the world, while the ministry of the ordained was appropriately spiritual and thus ordered to the Church. In fact, the priestly, prophetic, and kingly ministry pertains to the Church and not to the world. By initiating this move, the Council Fathers opened the door to the ministry of lay men and women *within* and on behalf of the Church. Lay people as well as the ordained now have a specific role in building up the Church, and not only in the secular world.

> Christ the Lord, High Priest taken from among men, made the new people "a kingdom and priests to God the Father" (Rev. 1:6). The baptized, by regeneration and the anointing of the Holy Spirit, are consecrated as a spiritual house and a holy priesthood, in order that through all those works which are those of the Christian man they may offer spiritual sacrifices and proclaim the power of Him who has called them out of darkness into His marvelous light. Therefore all the disciples of Christ, persevering in prayer and praising God, should present themselves as a living sacrifice, holy and pleasing to God. Everywhere on earth they must bear witness to Christ and give an answer to those who seek an account of that hope of eternal life, which is in them.
>
> —*Lumen Gentium*, 10

5. *The Universal Call to Holiness*

A fifth significant shift occurred when the Council drafted the chapter in *Lumen Gentium* called "The Universal Call to Holiness." Earlier patterns of thought had separated reality into the temporal and the spiritual and relegated care of the secular dimensions of life to the laity while reserving care of the spiritual realm to the ordained.

This led to a perception that the spiritual life—spirituality—was, first of all, somehow separable from the rest of human existence; and secondly, was the special domain of monasticism and the ordained. In general, "spiritual perfection" was not widely pursued by the laity and was not particularly associated with that state of life. *Lumen Gentium* changed that perception entirely. By reintroducing the theology of baptism as the source of the call to mission, and by stressing the foundation of ministry in service and charism, by identifying the Church as the whole People of God, and by extending the ministry of Christ to all the baptized, the Council reversed the direction of centuries of experience for Roman Catholics. The way was paved now for lay as well as ordained Catholics to undertake an entirely new journey toward an entirely new experience of ministry in the Church.

6. *Recovering the Permanent Diaconate*

Before moving on, I refer to a development in the renewal of the practice and theology of ministry that should not go unmentioned. Following the direction of the Second Vatican Council, specifically *Lumen Gentium*, 29, the ministry of permanent deacon, which had gradually disappeared, was recovered. I know personally that this ministry has been a profound and welcome addition to the Church of Rochester, and I know that to be the case in other dioceses in our country as well.

Two significant shifts are associated with the diaconate, which deserve to be mentioned in connection with the emergence of lay ecclesial ministry. One is that for the first time in centuries, ministry in the western Church in the practical order became separated from celibacy. Permanent deacons are not required to be celibate. This fact led to the first experience for many Catholics of a "recognized" minister being part of a family. This has become a most important link in the growth and realization of ministry as not restricted to celibates alone.

This new ministerial reality also brought to the surface a difficulty that other Christian churches faced long ago: what to do about spouses. Diaconal couples speak freely of the tensions that can develop within a marriage. "For thirty years my husband and I have exchanged the sign of peace at mass," one woman said. "Now my husband is in the sanctuary and I stand here alone. I understand it, I support his call, and I mind it very much."

A second shift that emerged with the re-emergence of the permanent diaconate is the presence of ordained ministers also simultaneously maintaining secular careers, fully engaged "in the world" while assuming ministerial roles within the Church. The ages-old split between "Church and world," "secular and sacred," "lay and clergy," "temporal and spiritual" were all transcended to some degree by the implementation of the office of permanent deacon. This "new" post–Vatican II ministry helped in very practical ways to open the way for the emergence of lay ecclesial ministry.

7

Voices from the Vineyard: Charlotte Bruney

I have found that the Holy Spirit most often speaks to me through a human voice. An idea is planted, and through prayer begins to take root. This is how I came to ministry. Back in 1982, the priest who was then my pastor in Connecticut invited me to change careers. I was a high school mathematics teacher and a very active Church volunteer at the time. He asked me to consider entering into an officially appointed collaborative team ministry with him—a model used in the Archdiocese of Hartford in those days to team priests, deacons, nuns, and lay people in the ministry of pastoring parishes.

The whole idea sounded absurd to me then because at the time I had had no experience of lay people in such roles. I asked him frankly, "What would I really be able to do?" He then said to me words that I will never forget: "Charlotte, there was nothing I did today, short of the saying of Mass, that couldn't have been done as well or even better by you!"

Looking back, I consider that moment my call story. Fr. Dominic Valla saw something in me—some gift, some talent— he thought would benefit the Church. That day he planted the seed that has brought me to this stage in my life where I serve as a pastoral administrator in the Roman Catholic Diocese of Rochester. It took me several more years to answer that call, to make the decision to pursue a master's degree in pastoral ministry, and to leave my chosen career to work full-time for the Church. Once I did, I never looked back—even when a new archbishop decided to eliminate lay ecclesial ministers from parish leadership at the end of our first, supposedly renewable, terms. What I experienced was a shocking and hurtful development. Thankfully, I was free enough to consider relocating and sought out opportunities for answering God's call in other dioceses.

I find lay ecclesial ministry a unique privilege and an awesome responsibility, one that has brought me great joy and satisfaction for more than two decades now. I am so thankful that someone cared enough about the Church and me to issue such an invitation. There have been plenty of challenges to being understood and accepted in this role. I find that Roman Catholics have limited imagination when it comes to thinking of anyone other than a priest coming to minister to them. Having said that, I find that once people experience good pastoral care in their times of need, they are most accepting of the caregiver, Roman-collared or not.

Four years after being appointed the pastoral administrator of St. Vincent de Paul Church in Churchville, New York, I learned that the diocese would no longer be able to provide a priest for us to celebrate sacraments here between weekends. For many months, I worked hard to find retired or extern priests to preside for us at weekday Mass, two or three days each week. This proved to be quite difficult. Realizing this, an eighty-year-old gentleman who was a regular at daily liturgy pulled me aside one morning and announced: "We've been talking and we've agreed that we don't want you working so hard to get us a priest for weekdays. We've decided that you should say Mass for us!" Stunned, I laughed aloud and then realized that he was perfectly serious. I asked him if he wanted to have me excommunicated; he replied, "We'll just pull down the shades. No one will have to know but us!"

As absurd as the suggestion was, I found their acceptance of me in my role as their appointed pastoral leader quite affirming. This small, but faithful, community gathers every weekday morning for either Mass or a Scripture and Communion service (at this point, it matters not which it is) because it is important to them to begin their day in prayer, feeling nourished by the Lord, and supporting one another through their daily trials and challenges. They want to do this in their own worship space and choose that over driving several miles to pray with another community for the celebration of the Eucharist. I cannot see taking that away from them.

In my experience, I find that the people in the pews are more accepting of lay ecclesial ministry than are some of my ordained colleagues. When I was new in the diocese, one of my parishioners landed in a local hospital and was facing emergency surgery. I had the priest chaplain paged. He was incensed that I had dared to page him and told me, in so many words, to have my pastor contact him with this request; he was not going to "march" to my orders. No explanation of what my role was for the parish community would satisfy him. This is an extreme example of the kind of treatment lay ecclesial ministers sometimes receive from clergy, but unfortunately, it is not a rare example.

Roman Catholics need their priests, and ordained ministry is necessary and critical for the survival of our Church. Lay ecclesial ministers need to understand that for many Catholics, they will always be poor substitutes for a priest in almost every situation, no matter how skillful and talented they are.

As more and more lay ecclesial ministers take greater responsibility for parish life and ministry and the number of priests available to serve continues to decrease, I fear that the centrality of the Eucharist is in jeopardy. It is not ignorance. Our weekday assembly knows well the difference between Mass and a Communion Service. Still, they will choose to worship together, no matter who is able to lead. Many of the faithful will tell you that lay presiders often bring more energy and enthusiasm to their task of leading the community in prayer, are often better preachers, and are more intimately connected to the people's own lives and concerns. Consequently the people, though extraordinarily grateful for the gift of ordained ministry, are also becoming almost too satisfied with lay leadership. It is so clear to me that the question of who may be ordained is the most important question facing the Church today. Are we really willing to sacrifice the availability of the Eucharist on an altar of celibacy? Which is more fundamental to our Roman Catholic system of beliefs?

Lay ecclesial ministry is one of the most rewarding careers I can imagine. Being able to support others on their faith walks, to help them see God present with them in their suffering and to rejoice with them in their triumphs, is payment in itself. I would not trade this vocation for the world, and would say that—without reservation—to anyone who believes God is calling him or her into this vineyard.

However, making the choice to work for the Church comes at significant cost for lay ecclesial ministers. Unlike many seminarians and deacon candidates, most of us pay for our own education for ministry. Our salaries are far below what someone with a graduate degree could expect to earn in many other fields. I believe that is why we see relatively few lay men or single people in this field. It is difficult to support a family on such an income, and single lay ecclesial ministers are unlikely to be able to afford to buy a home or take nice vacations, etc., without the support of a second income, a religious community, or a substantial nest egg to fall back on. In my own situation, for example, at each new job I have accepted, my starting salary was less than I was paid at my previous job! I have had to live off past savings, which I have, at this point, pretty much exhausted. At times, I worry that I may never be able to retire comfortably, and then I let go of fear and put my trust in God to provide for me. It is a big leap of faith. But anyone considering ecclesial ministry as a career needs to enter into it with eyes wide open.

I would also tell anyone discerning a call to this vocation that in order to be effective, lay ecclesial ministers, like all genuine servant leaders, must park their egos at the door. At times, you will feel invisible. Even though you may do the lion's share of the work for an event, such as preparing a family for the funeral of a loved one, or developing a penance service, the priest will get all the credit and all the praise and will sometimes act as if he deserves it. Know that God is aware of your efforts and will be eternally grateful! Take quiet pride in your accomplishments; that will have to be enough for you.

8

The Bishop and Lay Ecclesial Ministers

W hat is and what ought to be the relationship between a bishop and the lay ecclesial ministers who serve in his diocese? This is a crucial question. My brother bishops and I have expressed a desire for greater clarity and certainly more discussion. Lay ministers, as well, want and need greater clarity. This is so that all might better understand and appreciate their role in the local Church and, most importantly, that we are true to the best traditions of our faith. And this greater clarity will serve us well in the future as this significant development in the Church grows. Indeed, many of my brother bishops, and I as well, seek to establish a vital, ongoing relationship between us and lay ecclesial ministers as a necessary and welcome ingredient to the very life and mission of the institutional Church in the times to come. Certainly their numbers and significance in leadership will continue to grow.

As it stands now, the Catholic Church experience of lay ecclesial ministry is too fresh and still evolving for much to guide us definitively. However, it is good to have some kind of template, if you will, that informs and guides us, that propels us forward from a solid footing.

This template is the Church's own self-understanding as taught by the Second Vatican Council, more recent magisterial statements, and the work of theologians who help us deepen our appreciation of these teachings. I also believe these rich resources of conciliar, post-conciliar, and theological reflection allow for the kind of review and evaluation that will help keep the relationship between bishops and lay ecclesial ministers alive and growing.

As the late Pope John Paul II reminded us in his exhortation on the lay faithful,

> Communion and mission are profoundly connected with each other; they interpenetrate and mutually imply each other to the point that communion represents both the source and the fruit of mission: Communion gives rise to mission, and mission is accomplished in communion.
>
> —*Christifideles Laici,* 32

The late Holy Father tells us that communion and mission and ministry are inextricably intertwined. Put another way, all relationships in the Church are both personal—because we are in communion with each other—and ministerial, because our communion is directed toward mission. The bishop serves by virtue of his office as the propagator and fulcrum of this unity.

Like his relationship to priests and deacons, a bishop's relationship with lay ministers cannot exist in the abstract and is real only insofar as it is expressed in a loving communion focused on the work of the Church: spreading the Good News, gathering into community, worshipping God, and serving those in need.

One concrete way in which bishops are already involved in the work of lay ecclesial ministers is in the attention and resources we bring to their formation. In the United States we have a long history of providing a full seminary education for candidates for the priesthood, and in dioceses that have reinstated the permanent diaconate, non-residential formation programs have also been provided. In the case of the formation of lay ecclesial ministers, though tuition assistance is often available, truly adequate financial support has for the most part been lacking.

Those preparing for pastoral positions as lay ecclesial ministers in the Diocese of Rochester have been responsible for their own tuition and other expenses. This is difficult for many; it can be particularly difficult for some who have not developed independent incomes on their own because of family responsibilities.

I have spoken with women whose desire to undertake formation for ministry had to be abandoned because of the unwillingness of their husbands to support their study. Whether it is just for ordination candidates to enjoy full diocesan support for education while lay ministry candidates assume much or most of the cost for their education calls for further conversation. Likewise, our determination of whether this continued practice will—in the long run—serve the Church's need for well-prepared lay ministers remains to be seen. In the meantime, many dioceses, like our own, try to make at least some financial aid available for those who enroll in master's degree programs in ministry formation.

Programs of study for lay ministry have been evolving for some years, in a variety of settings. Because candidates for lay ecclesial ministry are often older, married with families, residential formation programs akin to those provided in seminaries are not prominent. Instead, some programs are housed in existing seminaries with the lay candidates enrolled in their own track, sometimes while taking classes with seminarians. Other programs have emerged as part of college and university theology departments. Access to such programs is often difficult for ministry candidates, since many are already established in careers and jobs, and sometimes the programs are located at significant distances from their homes. In this case, more and more Web-based courses and programs are emerging.

Co-Workers in the Vineyard of the Lord provides much encouragement and direction for bishops regarding the preparation of lay ecclesial ministers. To a great extent the document adapts the holistic formation programs outlined for priests (*Program of Priestly Formation*) and deacons (*The National Directory for the Formation, Ministry, and Life of Permanent Deacons*). This framework addresses the mandates of spiritual, pastoral, human, and intellectual formation. So, rather than a purely intellectual formation program that would focus exclusively on academic training in theology, *Co-Workers* identifies the fuller formation model required for priests and deacons as the ideal for lay ministers as well.

I am aware of the challenges this more expansive model poses for faculties. Instead of the single-gender, unmarried, and full-time student bodies that compose our seminaries, ministry schools must investigate new models suitable to the formation of lay candidates—many of whom are married with families, already engaged in parish communities, and employed in a range of other careers and jobs. The formation needs of those called to lay ministry are still being identified, articulated, and responded to in systematic attempts to meet those needs. The creativity of theology and formation faculties in recognizing and adapting their programs to the new students is absolutely necessary.

Communication between bishops and these faculties is absolutely essential as well. The call, I think, is for openness— a willingness to explore how we can assist in the support (not only financial) of these students and the new programs. In a way, this new movement in our Church that is returning us to an ancient identity is a blessing for us as bishops. It is one area where real growth is occurring, where new roles are being identified, where a real sense of excitement about the Church is the order of the day. How wonderful, really, for us to be a part of the birth of this new era of Church life!

This, of course, is not left to chance or happenstance. The bishop has the special responsibility of overseeing and coordinating the good order and functioning of ministry within his diocese. This is an aspect of all ordained leadership that requires a special emphasis today. Roger Cardinal Mahony and the priests of the Archdiocese of Los Angeles stressed this point in their pastoral letter on ministry, *As I Have Done for You*: "The ordained guides by establishing, cultivating and sustaining patterns of relationship rooted in equality, interdependence and mutual service . . . calling forth and coordinating the gifts of all the baptized." Clearly, this leadership extends to both pastors and bishops. In a particular way for our discussion here, this style of leadership is required in a bishop's relationship with those called to lay ecclesial ministry.

The episcopal function of overseeing ministry is at the service of communion. There is nothing closer to the heart of a bishop or more at the core of his responsibility than the unity of the Church. He has a particular responsibility to promote the unity of his own local Church in faith and love because he is called to be the inspiration and foundation of that unity.

At the center of his vocation, the bishop strives to preserve communion among the various vocations and ministries, protects their distinctive character, and officially designates ministers for a particular service, both ordained and lay. For all these reasons, I have used in the Diocese of Rochester the term "ministerium" for some years now. By this term, I mean all those who exercise in the local Church an official ecclesial ministry, whether they are ordained or not. By fostering a sense of ministry at this level, I believe the bishop can more readily form a relationship with lay ecclesial ministers—as he does with presbyters and deacons. He can also help such ministers avoid the temptations of individualism and parochialism, the antidote to which is precisely this sense of a diocesan ministerium to which they belong together with the clergy and to which they hold some greater degree of accountability.

To this end, we have held for the past three years an annual "Gathering of the Ministerium," well attended by hundreds of our priests, deacons, and lay ecclesial ministers. These daylong events center around a variety of topics and trends in ministry. They are not only informative, but create a sense of togetherness, of mutual purpose, and of communion among all those present.

I cannot stress enough the need for all, especially for a bishop, to foster this sense of communion in purpose. If we are to faithfully see this relatively new and most helpful rise in lay ecclesial ministry through its infancy, we must do it without friction and with our common mission always in mind. In an article I wrote some time ago for the *New Theology Review*, "On the Pastoral Exercise of Authority," I stressed this precise point.

> Most certainly, the Church is not a collection of individuals, each pursuing holiness on his or her own. It is the People of God, the body of Christ, a community of faith and love. In service to this community, a bishop must provide for good order while still respecting the freedom and supporting the growth of its individual members. As a true servant, he stands in the midst of a community to give his very self as a symbol of its unity and a guarantee of its peace. He preaches and celebrates the mysteries as friend among friends. Presiding in

> love, he helps the community to articulate its faith
> and reach consensus about its pastoral goals. He
> proclaims the vision of the whole, not as the lonely
> prophet, but as the one who clothes with words
> what he sees and hears in the hopes and dreams of
> the people he serves.
>   —*New Theology Review*, August 1997

If I were to summarize this episcopal role within the diocesan ministerium, I would say that bishops are responsible for
discerning, fostering, ordering, structuring, and empowering
the gifts of qualified ecclesial ministers on behalf of the local
Church over which he presides.

If the theory or framework of our relationships is important, no less important are the ways in which we live them out.
We need structures of communion—organizational mechanisms that help ensure that ministry in communion thrives
in fidelity to the Spirit's gifts. But whatever structures might
emerge to formalize the relationship between bishops and lay
ecclesial ministers, none will succeed if they do not spring
from the Church's own nature understood as communion in
mission and mission in communion.

If such structures are not in place, I fear that Zeni Fox's
pressing question, in her book *New Ecclesial Ministry*, will
remain unanswered and her warning unheeded.

> If lay persons exercise significant leadership in the
> Church, what is their social place? If it is not in
> some way with other official ministers, bishops,
> priests, and deacons, their understandings, values,
> and attitudes will not be influenced by those rela-
> tionships. (And conversely, neither will the other
> official ministers be influenced by them.) Further-
> more, over time many will experience anger at
> the marginalization they experience in relation to
> the other formal leaders in ministry. . . .Without

> identification as well with the larger body of offi-
> cial ministers, fragmentation rather than unity is
> fostered. Because a primary function of the bishop
> is as the center of unity within his diocese, it is
> the establishment of a formal relationship with the
> bishop that will contribute to a greater unification
> of all the official ministers in the local Churches.
> In a Church striving to be collaborative, such unity
> is essential.
> — *New Ecclesial Ministry: Lay Professionals*
> *Serving the Church*, p. 250

Of course, it would be naive to think that there could ever be just one right way to structure ministerial relationships. Circumstances differ from place to place. Boston is not Rochester. Dallas is not Chicago. And so on. Each diocese has its own history, priorities, resources, problems, possibilities, and dreams. We know that no two bishops, no two local Churches, are exactly the same.

One of the questions that is emerging in our own Diocese with considerable intensity, I think, is the role of one ministry in particular: the lay minister who is the leader of the parish according to the provision of Canon 517 §2. In my own diocese people in this role are called "pastoral administrators." In other dioceses the title of this position is different. In Albany, for example, this role is termed "parish life director," or "parish life associate." Other dioceses use other titles. At any rate, questions have arisen that are particular to those who take on this role. One such question concerns the liturgical role of the lay pastoral administrator, especially when an ordained sacramental minister is presiding.

We know that across history there has emerged a deep connection—theologically, ecclesiologically, and certainly at the level of feeling and perception—between the person responsible for the pastoral care of the local community and the one who presides over that community's Eucharistic celebration. This connection is almost part of the very fabric of Catholicism. Yet as bishops have appointed increasing numbers of lay ecclesial ministers to lead parishes, the liturgical role for such individuals is not yet defined. We know that the Code of Canon Law foresees the appointment of non-ordained ministers by providing for the very possibility of a bishop to entrust "the pastoral care of a parish . . . to a deacon or to some other person who is not a priest or to a community of persons" (Canon 517 §2). But what this law, and our current practice, does not offer is any provision of a liturgical role for the lay pastoral administrator or parish life director where so titled.

As the faithful have grown increasingly accustomed to the appointment of lay pastoral administrators, they are increasingly aware, too, that there is a defined and noticeable disconnect when it comes to the liturgical roles associated with the position. Both parishioners and pastoral administrators might expect the administrator—as pastoral leader of the community—to do things like walk beside the presider in the entrance procession and then to sit beside him in the sanctuary. Because the pastoral leader is so obviously charged with the spiritual care of the community, many see that these liturgical positions and gestures should follow from that very role. Concern that distinctions between the role of the priest presider and the lay pastoral administrator will be blurred by such practices has contributed to the emergence of a variety of policies that expressly forbid these practices.

The difficulties for me, as bishop, in welcoming this new role into our diocesan and parish life are made more numerous and perhaps more pronounced because of this disconnect within the liturgy between the role of spiritual and pastoral leader of the parish community and the one who presides at Eucharist. I hear, for example, from young parents who describe the meaningful and important relationship they begin to form with their pastoral administrator as they undertake preparation for their child's baptism. The pastoral administrator is indeed, for them, the pastoral and spiritual leader of their parish, and of their family. So when they approach the baptismal font on the day of their child's welcome into the community, it is natural that they expect the pastoral administrator to take some role in the rite. Again, this is forbidden at the present time. It would seem that at least the preliminary parts of the rite, such as the opening questions, could be conducted by the pastoral administrator. He or she is indeed the one who will call these same children by name into and in that community of faith.

A pastoral administrator described the disappointment of her parishioners at a confirmation liturgy held among five rural parishes in our diocese. She was the only pastoral administrator in that cluster, she was the only woman minister present there, and she was the only parish leader not present in the sanctuary that evening. She had come to know the ropes and was not at all troubled by the arrangements she had grown accustomed to and had grown to accept. But the parishioners from her parish were very upset. They found the arrangement hurtful and in some way diminishing of their community, and certainly of their leader. As we continue to nurture lay ecclesial ministry, we will absolutely need to recognize and assign the lay leader charged with a community's pastoral care an appropriate and clearly visible role within the community's worship. And we must foster among our leaders, lay and ordained, a greater sense of cooperation, mutual recognition, and collegiality.

In the Diocese of Rochester, where I have been bishop more than thirty years, we have tried in a number of ways to foster a sense of communion and a team philosophy among all of our ministers, ordained and lay. Please understand that these ways have not been universally popular. For example, in addition to the Gathering of the Ministerium I mentioned earlier, for several years now we have invited our deacon and lay pastoral administrators to our annual convocation of priests because it is there that we address the common pastoral problems facing those who have oversight of parish communities. This has caused discomfort to a few priests. I understand the reasons for this discomfort, but have proceeded anyway because I sincerely believe that the majority of our priests do not share these feelings and, more importantly, that it is crucial we begin somewhere to acknowledge the importance of our lay leadership by involving them in our planning, strategizing, and working toward a common purpose.

But above all, in all that we do, we must strive for more than a theology, however sound, and more than structures, however useful. We need a deep spirituality to sustain us. While all I have said about the relationship between bishops and lay ecclesial ministers derives from the ecclesiology of communion that is the hallmark of the Second Vatican Council, this cannot remain at the level of doctrine, nor of merely practical directives. Spirituality must enliven the council's vision of the Church.

In an apostolic letter marking the conclusion of the Jubilee Year 2000, Pope John Paul II spoke movingly of a "spirituality of communion" that should govern the Church, whose ministry is to be a sign and instrument of unity. Indeed, the Holy Father insisted upon this.

> Before making practical plans, we need to promote a spirituality of communion, making it the guiding principle of education wherever individuals and Christians are formed, wherever ministers of the altar, consecrated persons, and pastoral workers are trained, wherever families and communities are being built up.
>
> —*Novo Millennio Ineunte*, 43

The pope went on to say,

> The unity of the Church is not uniformity, but an organic blending of legitimate diversities. It is the reality of many members joined in a single body, the one Body of Christ (1 Cor 12:12). Therefore the Church of the third millennium will need to encourage all the baptized and confirmed to be aware of their active responsibility in the Church's life. Together with the ordained ministry, other ministries, whether formally instituted or simply recognized, can flourish for the good of the whole community, sustaining it in all its many needs: from catechesis to liturgy, from the education of the young to the widest array of charitable works.
>
> —*Novo Millennio Ineunte*, 46

I believe this kind of spirituality, so strikingly and challengingly put forward by our late Holy Father, is a vital necessity if a bishop is to serve as the reference point for the "communion in mission" of all members of his diocesan ministerium.

9

Voices from the Vineyard:
Anne-Marie Brogan

As pastoral administrator of St. Mary's Church in downtown Rochester, I have been blessed with the responsibility for the pastoral and administrative care of a Roman Catholic community of nine hundred families. The community gathers for worship in a beautiful city-center church. I collaborate with a talented pastoral staff, including a priest who serves as sacramental minister.

I can't imagine a better place to be. We are in a city that is showing such positive signs of new life. We follow a Church tradition that has, despite reports to the contrary, a rich and beautiful wealth of spirituality, theology, and liturgy. Lastly, we are in a diocese that has a courageous and encouraging leader in Bishop Matthew Clark.

Traditionally, of course, the leader of a parish would have been an ordained priest. Only an ordained priest may preside at Eucharist, give absolution, or anoint the sick. This is the way things are, but as a lay pastoral leader, I do not feel less capable in serving the community in most other ways. Readily we seek to offer care, compassion, and spiritual guidance, as well as teaching and administrative leadership.

At St. Mary's, the pastoral team, lay and ordained, work well together in a Church we love. We serve the varied needs of our community and others who seek support. But things have not always been this easy. Through the years I have had to face and move through—with the grace of God—many trials.

Being a lay ecclesial minister has been hard when:

- I have not felt accepted by some priests, deacons, or other companions at the table;
- I have been told that I can't possibly be called to pastoral ministry as a woman;
- I have prepared someone for marriage, and then the service is presided over by someone who does not have a relationship with the couple;
- my ability to do my job is questioned;
- people assume that the sacramental minister is the decision maker for the community;
- we lay ecclesial ministers are not offered equivalent professional, medical, academic, and social supports as ordained leaders of parish communities.

Being a lay ecclesial minister is wonderful when:

- I rejoice with a family over the birth and baptism of a new child;
- I experience the blessing of being able to get to the heart of what love is in conversation with an engaged couple;
- I look into the eyes of a dying person and see the light of God's love shining through;
- many people work together in the name of the Gospel and produce a life-changing response to a need;
- a staff member excels in ministry;

- people gather for the Eucharist;
- the Easter Candle is lit at the Vigil;
- lay and ordained work together in joy and mutual respect.

I thank God for this time at St. Mary's and dream of continuing to grow in my ministry—serving God, people, Church, and city with integrity—knowing that my call is valued and respected.

10

Women in Ministry

As we reflect on the emergence of lay ministry, the experience of women obviously merits special comment. In the United States and around the world, many Christian denominations have begun to include women among those who may be ordained. Naturally, this evolving ecclesiology has an impact on our own Church, and on all our lay ministers, whether female or male.

Before I continue, let me state clearly that I assent completely to the definitive teachings of Pope Paul VI and Pope John Paul II that the Church, following the example of Jesus in choosing only male apostles, cannot alter this pattern.

My loyalty to these teachings notwithstanding, I must also point out that many of us in church leadership have encountered both men and women who struggle with our Church's teaching regarding ordination. I have personally spoken with many women in the last few decades who, like St. Thérèse of Lisieux, testify to their sense of a personal call to ordained ministry. They find this a difficult cross, given the clear teaching of the Roman Catholic Church on the question of ordination. In fact, as we consider the reality of lay ecclesial ministry, we have to recognize that for women, their lay status is actually and inextricably tied precisely to their being women. This reality adds another level of spiritual and vocational challenge for lay ecclesial ministers who are women.

Clearly, many women testify to the contradictory nature of their experience in this regard. While every single female minister with whom I have spoken makes it clear that she finds her work in this capacity rewarding, and while we all see women ministers providing competent, skillful, and joyful service as lay ministers, the painful question of ordination affects many of them very deeply.

For some, lay ecclesial ministry has become a substitute ministry for the one to which they feel called. Women recognize the gifts they have been given, they acknowledge the call to ministry they have received, they cherish the Church and their own commitment to its life and mission. They see in lay ecclesial ministry the means by which their gifts are presented to the Church and their call to serve Christ is realized. The fact that ordination is not open to them is experienced as a restriction, and sometimes as a very real source of grief and anger. It is clearly a very real part of the challenge that ministering in today's Church presents for them.

At the same time, however, I have spoken with many women who, in spite of the struggle that this presents for them, work very hard to transcend their sense of restriction and their grief, so much so that the very denial of ordination can actually be, at times, encountered as a gift in terms of their experience as lay ecclesial ministers. For these women, the experience of a pilgrim community striving to realize the vision of Vatican II provides personal support and spiritual encouragement, in spite of what they see as an unfinished agenda. Without denying the difficulties that affect them in terms of ministerial identity, acceptance, and recognition, their connection with Christ is enriched, and their commitment to ministry is actually intensified.

In this regard, I am in admiration as I witness the transition now underway in some parishes of our diocese: the first generation of female lay ecclesial ministers is handing on their mantle of service to a new generation—those who take up their own call to ministry, having witnessed and shared in their sisters' service in the vineyard. This is the first generation about whom this can be said. These newest ministers will continue to build on the traditions begun by their sisters in ministry. New paths have been forged for them. Women before them have earned the first academic, theological, and ministerial degrees and have been involved in crucial ways in parish ministry. These dedicated pioneers have dealt with the skepticism of parishioners not accustomed to women in Church ministry.

As the torch is being passed to the new generation of female pastoral ministers, we do well to acknowledge some of the helpful practices our pioneers have established, as well as something about the tasks that remain as women continue to accept new roles as lay ecclesial ministers. In terms of the practices that have developed, I am aware of the importance that individual women assign to connecting with other women who are also willing to break new ground in the practice and theology of ministry. Connecting their own experience with that of others has sustained many women in ministry and nurtures their creativity and dedication. The traditional supports that have been available to priests are often missing for lay ministers, and for women in particular. But structures, both formal and informal, need to be developed to help people move beyond feeling alone in their vocations. I have found that our women ministers are the ones who initiate various types of support groups, whether focusing on issues pertaining to ministry, opportunities for spiritual enrichment, or providing a form of personal interaction and support. However such support mechanisms arise and are structured, they seem necessary and beneficial. It is important for me and my brother bishops to provide whatever support we can for encouraging women to find the means to benefit from such gatherings.

The influence of contemporary feminist and liberation theologies has also become an important source of help for women as they come to appreciate and celebrate their ministry and its role in forging the Church of the future. The prophetic traditions of scripture, theological and ecclesial themes relating to the People of God from the Council, and commentary by contemporary theologians all provide important sources of encouragement for women in ministry today. Patterns of alienation are distressing in American society as a whole. These developing strains from the theological reflection of our own culture and cultures across the world are sustaining and encouraging for women ministering in our Church today. As we anticipate the new leadership forms that are likely to characterize the Church in future centuries, we all benefit from these sources of reflection on the theological realities of our time.

In this connection, I offer two personal accounts, only because they illustrate something of the situations faced by all ministers, but especially by women. The first is a very simple illustration: a pastoral associate described for me her regular experience of interaction in the sacristy prior to weekend liturgies. As the priests and deacons, acolytes, readers, and Eucharistic ministers gather, she observes a pattern of interaction among the ordained ministers, particularly in which their greetings and comments—all largely informal and lighthearted— are nevertheless most often directed to one another. Thus she, an equal and a peer by competence, preparation, and appointment, is more often than not left feeling that she has is an outsider, somehow able to be set aside, in the society and camaraderie among co-workers. In many ways, this experience is not unexpected. Still, as we move forward in realizing the vision of what lay ecclesial ministry can mean, we will have to work hard to overcome some of the barriers among our co-workers. In the future, even the most informal structures of Church life and ministry will have to strive for new ways to exercise and witness to the inclusive nature being introduced by the realities of lay ecclesial ministry.

Some of the paradox of lay ministry in our country is exemplified in a difficulty involving more formal and structured limitation, a difficulty that affects women who have specialized in chaplaincy or pastoral counseling. For hospital and some other types of ministers, as well as pastoral counselors, the professional organizations for their support and accreditation often do not admit those who are not ordained.

This presents an anomaly for Catholic lay ministers, who are as qualified by training and competence as are their ordained counterparts from other denominations. Still, because of their lay status, membership in the professional organizations is not open to them. For those Catholic women who believe themselves called to ordained ministry, this situation seems to present a second source of loss and diminishment. Several have mentioned this to me. Even apart from the effect of this aspect of lay ministry on women, it demonstrates how the entire development of lay ecclesial ministry in our Church presents challenges in a variety of arenas as our entire concept of ministry, across a variety of faith traditions and professional organizations, changes to adapt to this new phenomenon.

11

Voices from the Vineyard: Deb Housel

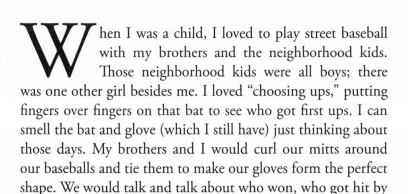

When I was a child, I loved to play street baseball with my brothers and the neighborhood kids. Those neighborhood kids were all boys; there was one other girl besides me. I loved "choosing ups," putting fingers over fingers on that bat to see who got first ups. I can smell the bat and glove (which I still have) just thinking about those days. My brothers and I would curl our mitts around our baseballs and tie them to make our gloves form the perfect shape. We would talk and talk about who won, who got hit by the ball, who ran the fastest, and the numerous windows that got broken over the years.

I loved the game and I loved playing it with my brothers, though it came with disappointments for me, as well. The largest was always wondering if I could be on the team that day or not. See, I could be on a team only if the team was short a boy. I was the fill-in player if a boy didn't show. Even though I could run faster than some, catch and pitch as well, I needed a male player to be missing in order to play. Sometimes one of my brothers would stay home just to make it so I could be on the team that day! Even though this may have been disappointing for me, I still loved baseball and wanted to be a member of the team. The love of the game was in me!

Just as the young girl baseball player in me who prepared my bat, ball, and mitt nightly to be ready in case I could be a member of the team the next day, I have prepared to answer the call that God offers me. God willing, acceptance will grow in the hierarchy of the Church and among the people in the pews.

It has not always been so. My adventure into lay ecclesial ministry began when I volunteered to prepare a group of teens for confirmation in 1987. I chose to do a visual prep by taking them on a tour of the Catholic Church. We took a train to New York City and visited St. Patrick's Cathedral, Covenant House, and Mother Theresa's soup kitchen. Closer to home in our own Diocese of Rochester, we visited a home for women called Bethany House, the monks of the Abbey of the Genesee, and the Pastoral Center.

From there I was literally raised up out of the pews and invited to step into lay ecclesial ministry when the deacon, who also was the faith formation director, resigned. At the time, I was a parishioner at St. Michael Church in Newark, New York. I was asked by the parochial vicar to apply. The pastor, the late Fr. Ed Steinkirchner, was hesitant but "trusted the process" of the recommendation.

In truth, I didn't know where I was being led. I had worked in the corporate world doing government procurements; my spiritual life was personal and for my benefit alone. In joining Fr. Ed in "trusting the process," I found myself thrilled to be working and not disconnected from my own faith life—I could work and discuss spirituality, our faith, and our Church. I loved it! I felt like I found my niche.

That first step into ministry was just a beginning. Since that time, I have served as a youth minister, hospital chaplain, two different times as a pastoral associate working for a pastor, and as a pastoral administrator fully responsible for the daily spiritual and financial life of a parish. In each role, I realized that it hardly mattered in which position I worked, as long as I felt that was where I belonged. As much as I have cherished these roles and still do, and as much as I would recommend a similar course for those who hear the call, the experience has not been without personal and professional moments of discouragement.

In joy I remember the youths to whom I ministered. They taught me to listen, lead, and raise up communities. I took what they taught me and applied it in all of my work. They taught me that Jesus comes to wherever the person is and walks with him or her from that point. It was a very special time: it amazed me that I could have the privilege of being spiritual leader to our youth, and that, as such, the communities respected me for it.

Yet, as a pastoral administrator—doing the same work but for all generations—acceptance became much harder to win. The ministry became for some people a gender issue. I must admit that it hurt, that in all of my desire and call to help keep communities open, vital, and raised up, my anatomy became more important than my gifts or my spirit—the very same gifts that had garnered praise when I was youth minister. Once again, I felt like that young girl waiting to see if she would be allowed to be on the baseball team! If there weren't enough guys I was acceptable—yet neither situation had anything to do with my gifts or abilities—only my gender!

In the midst of my work as pastoral administrator, I tried to concentrate not on the rejection by some, but the many rewards of being the leader of a parish, of being able to provide a model of a parish in which a priest could preside at Mass and flourish in a ministerial role without the stress of administration, staff management, and finances.

The thrill and reward I receive from the privilege of raising up communities and watching yet another person wake up to a God that loves her or him is beyond words and surpasses the sorrow of gender bias. In my years of ministry, I have seen several follow me into lay ecclesial ministry and have helped them deal with the difficult realities they experience in their work. It is very obvious that many enter into lay ecclesial ministry not realizing the strains, but only following a call that can't be refused. I do recommend, and have recommended to others, the life and career of an LEM; but I also offer the caveat that, just as they will change others, they, too, will be changed.

I am enjoying the journey! I am awed by being in this time of our history, a time in which all can participate in creating the vision. Just being a part of this exciting time, of planting the harvest to come, is a blessing to me. Above all, I feel blessed to be a lay ecclesial minister, to be able to stand as the presence of God in difficult times. I enjoyed being a chaplain for this very reason. Author Paul Claudel wrote, "Jesus did not come to explain away suffering or remove it. He came to fill it with his presence."

As I write this now, I am a planning group liaison for the Diocese of Rochester, helping parishes through the complex realities of our time, consolidations, closings, visioning. I still consider myself a minister but sometimes wonder if others do. Still, I have few, if any, regrets. I have a great deal of support, which is crucial to all in ministry. Discernment, prayer, a sense of humor, a support group, and a mentor are necessities for all ministers (lay or ordained). My own support is diverse, reflecting the reality of where we are now as a Church: they are lay and ordained, married and single, men and women, of varying theological convictions.

As a wife, mother, and grandmother, I can say that a lay ecclesial minister in my situation must have a family that realizes your call to ministry and accepts it. While most people are off on Easter, Christmas, and numerous other days—like Saturday and Sunday—the minister is most often working. The family of a LEM has to adjust to and honor the call God has given. As for me, in my vocation of marriage, I am all the more blessed with a family that offers up for the LEM.

Looking in at the Church from the outside is much different from working within the Church. There are so many challenges and rewards, emotions and questions, energy and lack thereof, but always that step-back-perspective that shows the Holy Spirit desiring to work through it all.

12

Men in Lay Ministry

Our reflections on lay ecclesial ministry would be incomplete without some thoughts about the experience of men who have accepted the call and committed their lives to this vocation. Youthful ministers tell me that they are always peppered with questions about why they felt called to be a *lay* minister. "Why wouldn't you want to be a priest? You can do so much more!" Middle-aged married ministers are assaulted with a different kind of question, "Isn't it a shame that the Church doesn't allow married priests? You'd make a great priest!" Even buried in the compliments, the ministers hear reinforced again and again that they are really second-class ministers, not like those first-class priests. Long after St. Paul, we still struggle to value a variety of ministries; long after the Second Vatican Council, male lay ecclesial ministers are still an oddity.

Male lay ecclesial ministers are greatly outnumbered in the Church today by female ministers. This is partly because in the first generation of lay ministry, many religious women were the first to volunteer to serve; partly because many married women called to ministry were able to pursue theological degrees while their husbands continued to support their families; and partly because many men who felt called to ministry either pursued the priesthood, or if they were married, the permanent diaconate. Other men, who tried out lay ministry briefly, moved on because of their inability to earn a wage sufficient to support a family. This gender imbalance has led to its own set of problems.

Just as in the past everything was seen from a celibate male's perspective, now many parish staffs tend to understand ministry primarily from a female perspective. In the exact reverse of what we used to hear, some men now tell me that they feel very uncomfortable and out of place at large staff meetings when they are the only male present. Studies tell us that this feminization of ministry tends to discourage vocations to lay ministry among males because of the paucity of role models and the resulting impression that ministry is really women's work. Likewise, this feminization of ministry has a tendency to discourage male participation in the worship and service life of the ordinary parish if their pastoral ministers, greeters, lectors, and ministers of Holy Communion are mostly women. We need to take this perceived imbalance seriously and intentionally work hard to bring gender balance into our parish staffs. Fortunately, particularly among the lay pastoral ministers in my dioceses, we are seeing many more men step up for service, bringing a healthier balance all around.

The men who serve as pastoral administrators in our diocese do not seem to have any easier time transitioning a parish to lay leadership than do women. The first year for all such ministers remains pretty painful for all. Parish communities generally feel slighted, devalued, hurt that they have not been assigned a priest pastor and somehow blame the new pastoral administrator for the paucity of priestly vocations. Parish staffs in general find all pastoral transitions difficult but in our experience transitions to the leadership of a lay pastoral administrator are particularly difficult. On the one hand, it is gratifying that most of these difficulties are not caused by gender bias. On the other hand, we need to recognize these inherent difficulties and do all we can beforehand to minimize its pain. One male minister recently told me that if his wife ever knew all the difficulties he was experiencing in transitioning a parish to the leadership of a lay ecclesial minister—all the cruel remarks, all the things done behind his back—his wife would make him quit. It is his spirituality and commitment to ministry alone that makes him continue to serve.

Some men tell me that they struggle mightily in ministry, attempting to balance the demands of marriage and family life and the demands of ministry. In one sense, because our celibate male priests are theoretically always available to serve the people, this same pattern gets imposed on lay ministers as well. A few years ago, I read an interview with the wives of six Anglican priests who had been re-ordained and received into the Roman Catholic Church in Australia. When asked about the greatest difference between their lives as Anglicans and Roman Catholics, they responded without hesitation—"the inordinate demands made by the Roman people on their clergy." We burn out our ministers—male and female—without ever realizing that we do.

I have noticed among our younger pastoral ministers, particularly the males who represent the next generation of ministers, that there is a different mood and mindset from their older counterparts. Their questions and their approaches are entirely different. Their spirituality is quite unique; they are pious but in a brand-new way, yet in many ways different than their older counterparts.

Epilogue

Wﾠhat do I see down the road? I am optimistic about the future. In my view, the emergence of lay ecclesial ministry in the Church is not just a sign of innovation or revision but is a sign of true renewal and hope. I truly believe that it is a work of the Holy Spirit. But there is much more to be done.

We need to continually reflect on the experience of lay ecclesial ministers and on our experience of their ministry. We need to work on the areas outlined in *Co-Workers in the Vineyard of the Lord*: recruitment, initial and on-going support, relationships with bishops and other ministers of the Gospel, relationships with the people lay ecclesial ministers serve, and compensation.

In addition to these, I will highlight just a few areas where I think particular attention is needed as we progress into the future. These are somewhat practical, but clearly emerge from the more pastoral and administrative standpoint that I naturally assume.

1. Minority Populations and Lay Ministry

A matter confronting our own diocese and undoubtedly many others concerns the recruitment and formation of lay Catholics from minority cultures. As lay ecclesial ministry in our Church has assumed an enhanced sense of professionalism, making it similar to other professions like physicians, teachers, lawyers, and so on, the training for these ministries has become more advanced. Currently, many of the positions open to lay ecclesial ministers in our own diocese require a masters degree. Candidates who feel called to these ministries not only must find the financial means to undertake this type of education, but prerequisites often include a bachelor's degree. We know that an educated pool of ministers is a great blessing, and this training is one of the great strengths of the whole phenomenon of lay ministry.

I worry that this development almost excludes people of minority communities from pursuing a call to ministry because their backgrounds and level of academic preparation may not have prepared them for admission into graduate school and seminary programs. Furthermore, dioceses lack or are unwilling to provide the financial support that could help to overcome this gap, and I am aware of very few programs that exist to help provide the background instruction needed by people in this situation. Our agenda for the future needs to include the will to find ways to enable minority communities to engage robustly in preparation for ministry.

2. Younger Lay Ministers

The need for additional support for minority populations is paralleled, I think, when we consider the circumstances surrounding some of our younger lay ministers. I had the pleasure of speaking with several of our new diocesan ministers recently, some of them having completed college and their MA degrees in pastoral studies only this year. They spoke of a number of hurdles before them, one of which is the uniqueness of the choices they've made, compared to so many others of their generation. Today's twenty-somethings, unlike previous generations, are often not formally associated with Church life at all. This means that young Catholics attracted to lay ministry can feel isolated from their own peers in ways not experienced by previous generations of Church ministers. This sense of isolation is intensified, perhaps, because many of the colleagues of these young people are older Catholics, even a generation removed from them.

These factors are combined with the newness of lay ministry itself and the need for these young people to be willing to forge ahead on a new path unfamiliar and perhaps uncomfortable for the very people to whom they will minister. It is clear to me that one of the challenges we face is in finding ways to support our youngest lay ecclesial ministers in their call. They take up their call in a culture dramatically more secularized than in the past, making their task more complex and perhaps more difficult.

3. Formal Connection to the Bishop

A third area of attention for the future is the formal relationship between bishop and lay ecclesial ministers. I do not want to belabor this point, but as we examined in chapter 8, part of the unfinished agenda for us is establishing the appropriate connection between lay ecclesial ministers and their bishops. As we become more practiced in the experience of lay ministry and as our reflection on it continues and deepens, we will gain, I think, increased clarity on what this relationship means and how we can express, formalize, and ritualize it. But we must be willing to continue to study, reflect, and dialogue for this to be done well.

4. Theological Reflection and Study

Along these same lines, our ability to critique and guide current developments will need to draw on several key sources so that the theological foundations of our work in guiding lay ecclesial ministry is sound and productive. Insights from Christology, ecclesiology, anthropology, liturgy, and canon law will be needed as we continue to analyze and review developments in lay ecclesial ministry, priesthood, the diaconate, and the episcopacy. Continuing dialogue among theologians, ministry formation faculties, and pastoral agents is absolutely necessary if this work is to be done satisfactorily.

Assistance from Scripture scholars and historians will be important, too, as we uncover models from the past that might guide us in our acceptance of new types of ministry and to face questions we have not yet studied in any great degree. I wonder, for example, whether we have knowledge of ways in which couples may serve in joint appointments as co-leaders of our communities. I believe there also will be more focused reflection on the relationship between the secular and the sacred— particularly in terms of helping us move beyond the traditional separation of these, a separation that perhaps obfuscates how we appreciate and understand the full mission of the Church and its ministry.

5. Formation for Lay Ministers

As I noted above, formation programs will be a continuing area of interest and attention in the coming years. Developing appropriate curricula for still-evolving ministry education programs is increasingly challenging in the face of limited and reduced financial resources. Devising formation programs for people already established in mature patterns of relationship, skills, and commitments, many of whom are also well engaged in family life and/or pastoral ministry of some type, presents an even more daunting task. Catholic ministry preparation has always involved more than intellection preparation alone. *Co-Workers in the Vineyard of the Lord* continues this emphasis with its insistence on the four-fold model comprised of intellectual, pastoral, spiritual, and human formation. The challenge before us is to flesh out what these several aspects look like in the concrete as we strive to train the people who present themselves today for taking up the call to the ministries of the future.

If we can accomplish this work and much more besides— and I have no doubt that we can—in faith and with mutual respect, we can be a part of the continued growth of one of God's greatest gifts to the post-conciliar Church. As odd as it sounds almost a half-century after Vatican Council II, we really are in our infancy, in the earliest stages of construction, as we as a Church strive to define, understand, and form a theology for lay ecclesial ministry. We are drawing the blueprint even as we build, with faith that it is God who guides our pen.

"One of the central purposes of *Co-Workers* was to state clearly and unequivocally that lay involvement in the Church matters," my fellow bishop, Most Reverend Gerald F. Kicanas, said in addressing the National Association of Lay Ministry in 2008. "You are important. You make a difference. You will not go away. Lay ecclesial ministry is not just a stop-gap measure to fill in for a shortage of priests, but the full flowering of our theology of communion and mission."

I could not agree more. I have seen this repeatedly in the Diocese of Rochester as I have witnessed the incredible contributions of our lay ecclesial ministers in our parishes and ministries. I have been struck by their professionalism and their dedication. I have seen first-hand the fruits of this tremendous development in our Church, and I do look forward in hope as it continues to blossom.

In so many ways, of course, the flourishing of lay ministry could not come at a better time. The number of priests serving our parishes in this country continues to decline, down 30 percent since 1975. In that year, 59,000 priests served the Church in the United States; by 2008 that number had fallen to 40,580. At this point, one in every six priests serving in this country comes from abroad. Despite the decline in number of active priests, the Catholic population itself continues to grow, at a rate of more than seven hundred thousand per year. Clearly, for the vitality of the Church in the United States to continue, lay ecclesial ministry needs to thrive as well. Parishes of the future—and even now as we know—are likely to be served by clergy serving a number of parishes while much of the day-to-day life of the parish is led by lay ecclesial ministers. These ministers will, I assume, include the ministries we have now, but will expand to include new ministries not even named at this point! The adventure before us promises to be a rich and exciting one, filled with promise and the trust that inspires, sustains, and draws us forward in the hope of Christ Jesus.

Matthew Clark is the bishop of Rochester, New York. He was born and raised in Waterford, New York, entered seminary in Albany and was ordained to the priesthood in 1962. Following ordination Clark served as a parish priest and then as vice-chancellor in the Diocese of Albany. He studied at the North American College in Rome, where he also served as spiritual director, and at Gregorian University, earning advanced degrees in theology and canon law. Ordained bishop in May of 1979 by Pope John Paul II, Matthew Clark was installed as eighth Bishop of Rochester in June of the same year.

Founded in 1865, Ave Maria Press,
a ministry of the Congregation of
Holy Cross, is a Catholic publishing
company that serves the spiritual and
formative needs of the Church and its
schools, institutions, and ministers;
Christian individuals and families; and
others seeking spiritual nourishment.

For a complete listing of titles from

Ave Maria Press

Sorin Books

Forest of Peace

Christian Classics

visit www.avemariapress.com

ave maria press / Notre Dame, IN 46556
A Ministry of the Indiana Province of Holy Cross